Praise fc
God's Healing

"This is not only an incredible, invaluable study for anyone who has ever experienced grief; it's a study we all should do. In addition to preparing our hearts for the inevitable, it will teach us how to minister to those who grieve. Ron and Kathleen have given us a compassionate, comprehensive, courageous study of grief that will take us full circle in comforting others with the comfort of the One who promises us He will never give us anything we cannot bear."

—Kay Arthur, Co-Founder of Precept Ministries International, speaker, host of *Precepts for Life* radio and television programs, and award-winning author of over 100 books and Bible Studies

"Those who have lost loved ones often find themselves suddenly launched into a sea of grief, buffeted by the wind and waves, tossed about helplessly with no sense of direction, convinced life can never be good again. Pop culture theology and well-intended platitudes only add to the confusion. Ron and Kathleen do an excellent job of pointing those who grieve to the only true source of comfort and direction, the Word of God. Through inductive study, they guide readers to discover truth for themselves, and show grieving people that though life will never be the same again, peace, hope, and even joy are still possible through a vibrant relationship with Jesus Christ. We recommend this for all who are mourning the loss of a loved one."

—Brad & Jill Sullivan, Co-Founders of *While We're Waiting* ministry to bereaved parents

"Some people say that time is what we need to heal in the midst of grief. But we need more than time—we need time spent hearing God speak into our pain and confusion. In *God's Healing in Grief* the Duncans help us as grieving people to hear and process God's Word so that deep despair can give way to genuine hope.

—Nancy Guthrie, Co-host of the Griefshare video series and author of *Hearing Jesus Speak Into Your Sorrow*

God's Healing in GRIEF

by
Ron and Kathleen Duncan

God's Healing in Grief

by Ron and Kathleen Duncan

© 2016 Ron and Kathleen Duncan

Published by Precept Ministries International

P.O. Box 182218

Chattanooga, TN 37421

www.precept.org

ISBN 978-1-62119-614-3

2016—First Edition

Printed in the United States of America

CONTENTS

To all who grieve.

Dear one, we understand your pain and sorrow. We've written this book for you. It came out of our experience with grief—grief over the loss of our parents, an aunt, a nephew, and many friends. But mostly out of our experience with grief over the loss of our son. And out of the amazing, beautiful grace and healing in Christ we have experienced. We have hope because of Christ.

Our prayer is that through this study you will find hope and healing in Christ Jesus as we have. We pray, too, that you will reach a place in your healing where you can share this hope with others who grieve.

> *But we do not want you to be uninformed, brothers, about those who are asleep, that you may not grieve as others do who have no hope. For since we believe that Jesus died and rose again, even so, through Jesus, God will bring with him those who have fallen asleep.*
> (1 Thessalonians 4:13-14)

> *More than that, we rejoice in our sufferings, knowing that suffering produces endurance, and endurance produces character, and character produces hope, and hope does not put us to shame, because God's love has been poured into our hearts through the Holy Spirit who has been given to us.*
> (Romans 5:3-5)

In Christ,

Ron & Kathleen

August 13, 2013…The Day Our Lives Changed Forever!

There was a knock on the door. It was 5:47am. I looked out the window and saw a cop car. Not good. Never a good thing to have a cop at your door. Worse this time of day.

I grabbed my bathrobe; Ron got up to get dressed.

Officer Wiggins had seen the news on the police wire and volunteered to come to our home with the news. He knew our family. His son had graduated just a few months before with our son Peter.

Officer Wiggins came in and told us our 20-year-old, Andrew, had been in a car wreck. Our son was dead.

I sat in the corner of the couch. Numb. My son was dead.

Our three children living at home had heard the door and the noise in the living room, and one by one they came in to ask what was happening. One by one we told them. One by one they each got off the couch and went back to their room. Their brother was dead.

I sat on the couch numb. My son was dead.

Ron called the other children to give them the news: one daughter on vacation with her family; our former Marine in Denver; our gymnastic coach son in Michigan. Their brother was dead.

While Ron called the kids, I got on Facebook to see if I could learn more. The local police knew very little. The troopers were still processing the scene. All they knew was that our son was dead.

One young man had posted kind words on Andrew's page. I sent him a message asking him to call me. He told me they had all been at the end-of-the-season cast party for "Texas" the day before. (This had been Andrew's second year in this outdoor musical. Andrew loved that show; he loved being a professional actor and dancer; he loved the cast and crew.)

On the way home from the cast party about 11:45 pm, six young people had been riding back to Canyon, Texas, when the driver ran a stop sign and pulled out in front of a semi. Andrew was killed along with four of his friends, including the driver. They were pronounced dead at the scene by a justice of the peace at 12:30 am. One person survived and was in critical condition. The driver of the semi was in serious condition. I had one question: "Was Andrew driving?" He was not driving . . . but he was dead.

I called my step-mom. Her grandson was dead.

Ron called more family. Their nephew, cousin, etc. was dead.

Ron contacted our pastor. A member of his congregation was dead. A youth from his youth group was dead.

I posted the following on Facebook and sent out an email to tell people their friend was dead:

> Our sweet, funny and talented Andrew Raymond went to be with Christ this morning about 12:30.
>
> He was riding in a car going back to Amarillo from the annual End of the Show Ranch BBQ with other cast members from "Texas." He and four others were killed when the car they were in was struck by a semi. One person in the car is in surgery. We do not know any other details at this time.
>
> Please pray for our family as we deal with this loss.
>
> Pray for the families of the others involved, including the driver of the semi involved. I pray that somehow God will be glorified in this.

I walked away from my computer. The next few moments were quiet and still. It would be a little while before anyone arrived at the house, before we could really do anything; we had to wait.

Ron and I talked a bit. We had plans to make; arrangements for our son's funeral needed to be made. We talked quietly.

We made a few decisions:

1. We would not blame the driver. It could have as easily been Andrew. Cast and crew had taken turns driving to events all summer. He could have been driving. Blame would not change things. It didn't matter to us if alcohol were involved. That would not have changed the outcome.

2. We would make it through this. We WILL make it through this together.

3. We would believe. The most important thing we discussed was this: **Our son was not dead!** Andrew was and is still alive! He is alive in our memories, in our love, in our home, in the thousands of pictures we have of him, in the hundreds of hours of video of him. He is alive!

More than that: the reality is that Andrew *is* not dead. He is now living in the presence of Christ. He will be dancing and worshiping before the throne of his

Savior for eternity! He is *even more alive than he ever was on earth!* And Andrew lived well here; he lived life to the fullest here on earth! But now he is living eternally with Our Heavenly Father.

My life changed forever that day. I had to deal with grief in a way I never dreamed. We had lots of things to take care of: lots of details, legal stuff, funeral stuff, closing accounts, shutting off his phone, cleaning his apartment, finding his car! It took a long time to work through details and legal stuff.

But one thing in my life didn't change and never will: God is the same yesterday, today and forever.

On August 12 God was a loving, compassionate God. He cared for me. He loved me. He had begun a work in me and promised to carry it on to completion until the day of Christ Jesus. He sent His Son to die for me. He promised to never leave me or forsake me. He was the King of Kings, the Lord of Lords, Creator, Redeemer, Messiah and my Friend.

On August 13 all those things were still true!

They still are true.

They will be true forever.

Even on remarkable days, some things don't change.

> *Heal me, O Lord, and I shall be healed; save me and I shall be saved, for you are my praise (Jeremiah 17:14).*

What Will this Study Do For You?

Though we had lost others, no event in our lives prepared Ron and me for the loss of our son. It was as if the death of a child was a murky theory, a remote possibility that happens to everyone else. We expected our children to live long, happy lives. We expected them to outlive us. When that doesn't happen, when the improbable becomes real, life gets dark and grim quickly. We need light in the form of short-term relief and long-term hope.

That's what we want to share with you. While there are many books on how to handle grief, the purpose of this one is to help you find healing, hope, peace, and joy once again, *even while* you're grieving, by reading and studying God's Word. This is how you can get to know your heavenly Father, the God of eternity, personally, develop a closer relationship with Him, and in doing so find the healing you desperately want and need.

God alone heals broken hearts. He promised to comfort those who mourn. In His Sermon on the Mount, Jesus said, "Blessed are those who mourn, for they shall be comforted" (Matthew 5:4)

This sounds promising, but those of us who have suffered through the loss of a child, spouse, parent, best friend, *still* have some pretty tough questions:

- What "comfort" can we expect from the Lord and how do we get it?
- How can I find joy and peace when my child, spouse, or parent is dead?
- How can we truly heal when the relationship we had can't go back to "the way it was"?
- Why did my loved one die? Why are others healed from the same sickness?
- I'm sad all the time; am I sinning?
- I'm angry at everyone who was at fault. What do I do now?
- Is my loved one okay? Is she in heaven?
- Did my loved one become an angel? Does he watch over me now?

The Bible has answers to these questions and many more. We'll guide you through your own study to find answers to these questions *for yourself.*

Many books do the work for you. Some of them help you understand the psychological impacts of loss but you need to be careful: many of them teach philosophies contrary to the Bible and in fact reject its teachings. Others combine biblical truths with errors, usually more fantasy than fact. How can you discern the difference?

By studying what the Bible says yourself!

We offer simple activities to help you get truth straight from God's Word. Together we'll address the tough questions above and others directly to relevant scriptures. This will gently lead you to the foundation of Jesus Christ—the rock-solid Base of all comfort, healing, and hope!

The first part addresses our need to have a relationship with God to deal with grief. But we'll first learn about who we're relating to. If we don't know God's nature and works we can't begin to heal. The second part addresses positive responses to grief in light of the hope God gives us for this life and for eternity. We learn how His Word transforms us into the image of Christ. Along the way we look the topics that most often come up when we deal with the death of a loved one. Finally, we observe the responses of several psalmists to God when they were tested and how these responses can help us heal.

Each lesson begins with an introduction to the topic. Often it will include a story and insights we learned from our own grief journeys. Then we look at passages from the Bible to see what God says about the topic. This is where inductive study comes in.

We'll ask you to observe the text carefully so it will speak to you directly. While we offer some opinions here and there, the study is designed for you to interact with God's thoughts yourself. The Holy Spirit will teach you; that's God's promise (1 John 2:27).

In each lesson you'll read passages of Scripture then answer questions to help you extract what God is saying. Often we'll advise you to mark key *words* like sorrow, grief, comfort, and God and pronouns that refer to them to highlight the author's emphasis on key *ideas* that enhance understanding. Markings help you relocate these ideas *quickly*. You can use a plain pencil or colored pencils to underline, box, circle, triangle, or just shade them. After this you'll want to list what you learned to seal these truths in your heart.

The next goal is to direct questions to texts to help you understand their meaning and then record your answers.

God wants us to apply His Word—the ultimate purpose of all Bible study. But how do I do this? What should I believe and how should I act? This may be the hardest part. Grief will often put a drag on our applications. That's okay! The good news is: the Holy Spirit will offset this, empower us all along the way.

The "way" is a long one so don't plan to rush by trying to complete a lesson a day. Plan rather on spending a few days in each. Take each slowly and steadily. Ask the Holy Spirit to show you the truth, beauty, and joy of God's Word.

As you walk through grief, you will have times when you need to simply be still and listen for God's voice. Other times you'll need to "offer up prayers and supplications, with loud cries and tears, to him who [is] able to save [you] from death" just as Jesus did (Hebrews 5:7). Some of the concepts in this study may be hard to digest. Work through them in your own time at your own pace. Ask the Holy Spirit to give you insight and comfort. If you need more than a week for a lesson, that's okay too.

We encourage you to work through the book with a group of friends who have experienced loss like yours. You can work through a lesson each week then come together weekly to discuss what you learned. In the back of the book you'll find a section titled **Using This Book for Group Discussions**.

Just Journaling

Throughout this study, you will find *Just Journaling* prompts. They're optional, but most people (starting with us) have found that journaling facilitates healing from grief. These prompts will cue you to think and record things like:

What or who I'm grieving

What I hope to gain from this lesson

How I'm feeling about what I just learned

Poems and prayers to express my thoughts about the lesson

[Kathleen] Writing about my feelings, thoughts, struggles, and successes helped me process my grief. My Journal is my blog. I write about my grief journey and what God has shown me in my private study time as well as in group studies. I share my struggles and failures; I write about the good things in my life and I write about my faith.

Consider using our companion volume "My Journal for God's Healing in Grief" or start one of your own (a simple notebook will do). Some of the questions in this book will take more space to answer than others. If we haven't given you enough room, write your answer in your Journal. You may want to express your thoughts in prayers, poetry, and/or drawings. You may want to compose a song that expresses your pain but also, eventually, your victories amid your grief journey.

You will have victories in grief, but grief itself is not something to be conquered, but rather it is something that is normal and natural, something we go through and feel when we lose someone we love.

Your Journal is a place where you can write your prayers to God the way the psalmists did. From my experience, a Journal to write or draw in is extremely helpful for processing grief and the accompanying emotions, thoughts, and questions. Be sure to date Journal entries so you can go back later and see how God worked in your life.

As we said at the beginning, the purpose of this book is to help you find healing through a study of God's Word.

Here's your first *Just Journaling* prompt:

Just Journaling

Begin to write about your thoughts and feelings in grief. You might want to start by writing about the loss you are grieving. Write about your loved one. Maybe include a picture or some of your favorite things about them.

Write down some of the questions you have about death, heaven, grief, and healing. What are you hoping to learn through this study?

Be honest in your Journal which is just between you and God. As we go through this study you will have opportunity to write in your Journal and look back to see what God has done in and through you.

LESSON 1

Comfort in Grief

¹ *I lift up my eyes to the hills.*
  From where does my help come?
² *My help comes from the* Lord,
  who made heaven and earth.

³ *He will not let your foot be moved;*
  he who keeps you will not slumber.
⁴ *Behold, he who keeps Israel*
  will neither slumber nor sleep.

⁵ *The* Lord *is your keeper;*
  the Lord *is your shade on your right hand.*
⁶ *The sun shall not strike you by day,*
  nor the moon by night.

⁷ *The* Lord *will keep you from all evil;*
  he will keep your life.
⁸ *The* Lord *will keep*
  your going out and your coming in
  from this time forth and forevermore.
(Psalm 121)

The loss of a loved one of any age and by any cause leads to pain and grief. Where can we turn for help and comfort when we are grieving? Who can comfort us in our grief?

Psalm 121 tells us that our help comes from the Lord, who made heaven and earth. It says "The Lord will keep you from all evil; he will keep your life." But for those of us who have experienced the death of a loved one, it may seem that the Lord did neither of these things.

We have experienced loss in many ways over the years. We buried our parents and grandparents. We helped care for two parents as they each died from cancer. Those deaths were expected. Those wonderful people had lived good, long lives, but it still hurt when they died.

We have also had friends who died in accidents and from addictions and illnesses. We had to bury our twenty-year-old son after he was killed in a car wreck along with four of his friends. And we have watched friends bury their parents or children.

All of us who have lost loved ones ask the hardest questions. "Is what I have been taught true?" "Did God keep us from evil?" "Did he keep our son's life?"

We know grief. We know the pain of losing people we love. We know the questions that often plague us in those early days of our grief journey.

We also know the healing and comfort that comes from the Lord. We have experienced it! We have found joy and peace even as we grieved those we lost. We know God does keep us from evil and He keeps our life. The keeping just may not look like what we thought it would look like.

For those of you early in your grief journey, we know you are still hurting. You may still be crying almost daily. You may be finding it hard to function. Whether the loved one you lost was a child, infant, teen, young adult, older adult or preborn child, the loss is painful. Some of you have lost your child, others a sibling, spouse, parent, family member, or friend.

Those of you farther along in your grief journey may feel like your lives will never be the same again. The truth is: they won't be. Someone you care for deeply is no longer alive on this earth. Something major has happened and it will change you. But if you ask Him, God can and will use all of this for His glory and your good. He is a compassionate, gracious God who loves you. He will heal your broken heart.

Each of us is unique. The people we lost were unique and special to us. Their lives were unique. Their deaths were unique. Our grief will be unique. But the source of healing for each of us is the same: Jesus Christ and Him crucified, buried, and risen from the dead!

Healing from the loss of a loved one does not happen quickly, certainly not overnight. But it can happen if you are honest and willing. It takes work, dear one. We must be honest and willing and we must work to find healing. It requires that we diligently seek the Lord and trust Him. We must study His Word and obey His commands. We must remain steadfast through this trial. There are great rewards for doing so:

JAMES 1:12

12 Blessed is the man who remains steadfast under trial, for when he has stood the test he will receive the crown of life, which God has promised to those who love him.

And God has given us the Holy Spirit, the Comforter, to help and teach us.

JOHN 14:26 (KJV)

But the Comforter, which is the Holy Ghost, whom the Father will send in my name, he shall teach you all things, and bring all things to your remembrance, whatsoever I have said unto you

Though we will miss our loved ones who have gone on before us, we can find peace and joy again, in Christ.

[Kathleen] There is a void in my life that only our son Andrew filled. I miss his laugh, his stomping through the house, his hugs, and his stories. Nothing will ever replace my son in my life. I still have moments and even days of sadness. Some memories still bring tears. I see his friends dance, graduate, get new jobs, and marry. Knowing I won't get to see Andrew do these things brings a twinge of pain. Yes, I will grieve the loss of my son until I die.

However, those early days of sorrow so deep that I physically ached are gone. The days of doubt, sobbing, and aching have passed. Seeing an old picture of all four of my boys together no longer takes my breath away. I no longer count the days, weeks, or months since I saw him last or since the date of his death. I no longer cry each time I see a picture of him or hear his name. I no longer wake up with my pillow wet from my tears. Death is no longer a central theme in my thoughts.

How did I reach this point? How was I healed from this deep level of grief? By turning to Our Heavenly Father and trusting in His promises. I had studied the Bible and understood many of them. He promises to comfort us, to be with us, and to love us. He is a gracious God, full of mercy and abounding in love. I reached this point by trusting Him and doing the next right thing.

The next right thing may be as simple as getting out of bed and getting dressed or it may be going back to church for the first time in a while. It may be going back to work, joining a Bible study, or taking care of your children. You don't have to figure out what tomorrow or next week will look like; you can simply do the next right thing today. You can apply God's truth in your life today. And in trusting God and doing the next right thing He will bring you to a place of healing and peace.

If you are willing, He will do the same for you. If you want to find peace, joy, and hope in the midst of your grief, the Holy Spirit will lead you to a place of healing and restoration.

Are you willing to let God work in you and lead you? If you are, begin with prayer and ask the Holy Spirit to teach you, comfort you, and lead you into a place of healing and peace. I know that for many of us in grief, prayer has become hard. You may not be sure how to pray anymore. Sweet friend, simply talk to God. Ask Him to teach you. Tell Him you are willing to learn. He is listening.

Losing a loved one is tragic. It is horribly painful. You may be angry because of your loss. You may have doubts and fears you have not shared with anyone. You may even find it hard to pray. Your prayer doesn't have to be fancy or long, but it should be honest. As we work through this study, be honest with God. Take time to tell Him what you are thinking and feeling, no matter how bad that is. He knows it already, beloved. He knows your heart, and He loves you.

1 CHRONICLES 28:9

> [9] *"And you, Solomon my son, know the God of your father and serve him with a whole heart and with a willing mind, for the Lord searches all hearts and understands every plan and thought.*

Just Journaling

Write out your prayer. Ask the Holy Spirit to teach you, comfort you, and lead you into a place of healing and peace. If you can, write what healing might look like to you. If you can't imagine healing and joy right now, that's okay. Be honest about your thoughts and feelings.

God's Comfort in Loss

As we look at Scripture together over the coming weeks, be open and honest with God. He knows your pain. He knows your sorrow. He knows your heart.

And He loves you.

Let's start looking at what the Bible says about God's comfort and His love for you. We will look at some of these passages again later in the study, but for now read the verses that follow and draw a triangle over *God* and *Father* and any synonyms such as *he, I,* or *you*. Draw a cross over *Lord Jesus Christ* or *Christ*.

Then read them a second time, this time circling the word *comfort* and drawing a teardrop over the words *afflicted* and *sufferings* and a heart over the word *love*.

For each verse, write what the Bible says about God's comfort and love for you. You may not be at a place where you believe these truths yet. That's okay, just look at what the Bible says about God, see what you can learn, and be willing to let Him teach you.

How does Paul describe God?

2 CORINTHIANS 1:3-7

³ *Blessed be the God and Father of our Lord Jesus Christ, the Father of mercies and God of all comfort,* ⁴ *who comforts us in all our affliction, so that we may be able to comfort those who are in any affliction, with the comfort with which we ourselves are comforted by God.* ⁵ *For as we share abundantly in Christ's sufferings, so through Christ we share abundantly in comfort too.* ⁶ *If we are afflicted, it is for your comfort and salvation; and if we are comforted, it is for your comfort, which you experience when you patiently endure the same sufferings that we suffer.* ⁷ *Our hope for you is unshaken, for we know that as you share in our sufferings, you will also share in our comfort.*

What does this passage say about God's comfort? Make a list of all you learn about comfort.

What is God's hope for you? What does He want you to share?

Notice that this passage says even the righteous have afflictions. What does it say about God? List what God does to help.

In the following verses, draw a triangle over *God* including synonyms and pronouns, a cross over *Christ,* and a teardrop over all words that show mourning. Write what you learn about God's comfort and love.

PSALM 34:17-19

¹⁷ When the righteous cry for help, the L*ORD* *hears and delivers them out of all their troubles.* *¹⁸ The* L*ORD* *is near to the brokenhearted and saves the crushed in spirit.* *¹⁹ Many are the afflictions of the righteous, but the* L*ORD* *delivers him out of them all.*

PSALM 56:8

⁸ You have kept count of my tossings; put my tears in your bottle. Are they not in your book?

PSALMS 147:3

³ He heals the brokenhearted and binds up their wounds.

LAMENTATION 3:22-24

²² The steadfast love of the L*ORD* *never ceases; his mercies never come to an end;* *²³ they are new every morning; great is your faithfulness.* *²⁴ "The* L*ORD* *is my portion," says my soul, "therefore I will hope in him."*

MATTHEW 5:4

⁴ Blessed are those who mourn, for they shall be comforted.

MATTHEW 11:28-30

²⁸ Come to me, all who labor and are heavy laden, and I will give you rest. *²⁹ Take my yoke upon you, and learn from me, for I am gentle and lowly in heart, and you will find rest for your souls.* *³⁰ For my yoke is easy, and my burden is light.*

1 PETER 5:7

⁵casting all your anxieties on him, because he cares for you.

Summarize what you learned about God from these verses. Make a list of what He is and what He does for us. Although this is redundant, the repetition will help you remember who God is and what He promises to do.

Isn't it beautiful? God promises to be near and comfort us who are broken-hearted! He comforts us through His Word, other people, the beauty in creation, and through the Holy Spirit who teaches us and guides us as we walk through the valley of grief. God promises to comfort us in our grief because He loves us.

Read the next verses. Mark *love* with a heart and draw a cloud around *eternal life*. Note what you learn.

JOHN 3:16, 36

¹⁶"For God so loved the world, that he gave his only Son, that whoever believes in him should not perish but have eternal life.

³⁶"He who believes in the Son has eternal life…"

ROMANS 5:8

⁸but God shows his love for us in that while we were still sinners, Christ died for us.

What is the result of God's love for us according to these verses?

Just Journaling

You've just looked at verses about God's love and comfort. How are you feeling about what you learned? Write your feelings and thoughts about God and His comfort in light of your loss. What impact do you think this understanding will make in your life?

Copy any verses you want to remember from this lesson in your Journal. Throughout this study you may want to write there verses that touch you in a special way.

Read 1 Corinthians 15:3-5. Mark *Christ* and all *synonyms* with a cross.

According to this passage what happened to Christ? What did He do? Make a list.

1 CORINTHIANS 15:3-5

³ For I delivered to you as of first importance what I also received: that Christ died for our sins in accordance with the Scriptures, ⁴ that he was buried, that he was raised on the third day in accordance with the Scriptures, ⁵ and that he appeared to Cephas, then to the twelve.

Continue to mark Christ. Draw a tombstone over the words *dead* and *fallen asleep*. Underline *alive*.

Because Christ has been raised from the dead, what is the result for those "in Christ"?

1 CORINTHIANS 15:20-22

²⁰ But in fact Christ has been raised from the dead, the firstfruits of those who have fallen asleep. ²¹ For as by a man came death, by a man has come also the resurrection of the dead. ²² For as in Adam all die, so also in Christ shall all be made alive.

Put a tombstone over the words *dead in Christ* and *fallen asleep*. Circle *hope*.

1 THESSALONIANS 4:13-17

¹³ But we do not want you to be uninformed, brothers, about those who are asleep, that you may not grieve as others do who have no hope. ¹⁴ For since we believe that Jesus died and rose again, even so, through Jesus, God will bring with him those who have

What do Paul, Silvanus, and Timothy want their readers generally to know?

According to these scriptures, what will happen to our loved ones who have died before us?

fallen asleep. [15] For this we declare to you by a word from the Lord, that we who are alive, who are left until the coming of the Lord, will not precede those who have fallen asleep. [16] For the Lord himself will descend from heaven with a cry of command, with the voice of an archangel, and with the sound of the trumpet of God. And the dead in Christ will rise first. [17] Then we who are alive, who are left, will be caught up together with them in the clouds to meet the Lord in the air, and so we will always be with the Lord.

What key term does Paul use to contrast the grief of believers and unbelievers?

Is this term no more than wishful thinking? What is it based on?

Have you noticed this difference in your own life and in others'?

In writing to the church at Thessalonica, Paul said he did not want them to grieve as those who have no hope. We can have hope because of who God is and what He promises us in His Word.

Because of His great love for us, God sent Jesus to die on the cross and rise from the dead so you and I can have eternal life. Eternal life begins when we first accept Christ. It means we will "always be with the Lord." What a comfort that is for us who have experienced the death of a loved one! All who believed in Jesus Christ and have died are alive and in His presence!

Read Revelation 21:1, 4. Underline what God will do for us:

REVELATION 21:1, 4

[1] Then I saw a new heaven and a new earth, for the first heaven and the first earth had passed away, and the sea was no more.

[4] He will wipe away every tear from their eyes, and death shall be no more, neither shall there be mourning, nor crying, nor pain anymore, for the former things have passed away."

If you want to learn more about heaven and what happens when we die, you may want to complete the 40-Minute Study "Heaven, Hell, and Life after Death."[1]

The promises in God's Word are our hope! Even when we grieve, we have hope. Though we suffer and grieve on earth now, a day is coming when the dead in Christ will rise and we will join them to meet the Lord! There will be no more sorrow and no more tears! What a glorious day that will be!

Now is a good time to write down some of your thoughts and feelings about your grief and your loss. What do you think it will look like to have healing in your grief? You may want to write a prayer. Be honest with God about your grief.

Beloved, God knows your heart and your thoughts already. He knows you have questions. He knows your pain. He understands and loves you. He wants to comfort you and give you peace. Speak to Him about your grief and any questions and doubts you have. He understands and He loves you.

As you work through this study our prayer is that you will find healing and hope even as you grieve.

---

[1] Kay Arthur, Bob and Diane Vereen, *Heaven, Hell, and Life after Death* (Colorado Springs, CO: WaterBrook Press, 2014).

ROMANS 15:13

May the God of hope fill you with all joy and peace in believing, so that by the power of the Holy Spirit you may abound in hope.

Just Journaling

In our Journal you'll find a chart titled "What I Learned About God." If you started your own Journal, then start a list with this title. We'll be coming back to it often. Then, go back through this lesson and add everything else you learned about God. As you go through the rest of this study, continue to add to this list. You may want to leave a few blank pages so you have lots of room to add to your list. This list will help you come to know more of who your Heavenly Father is, develop a closer relationship with Him, and in doing so find the healing, peace, and joy you seek.

LESSON 2

Why Study the Bible When I'm Grieving?

. . . give me life according to your word! (Psalm 119:25b)

Why did this happen?
Why did my loved one die?
Can I trust God?
How can I find peace and joy?
How do I think and act and live now?

These are difficult but good questions. You may not know the answers and most likely neither will your friends, coworkers, and social media contacts. Their advice, if not from the Bible, will be poor comfort, perplexing, and flat-out wrong. They may say you need to "find your own way in your grief" or "it's okay to do whatever helps you; it's your grief." They may offer platitudes like "Everything happens for a reason" or "God needed him more than you do."

We're sure you've heard "Time heals all wounds!" Friend, it's not true! Time spent doing the wrong things won't heal anything! God warns us against the works of the flesh (Galatians 5:19-21). If you spend time participating in works of the flesh such as sexual immorality, idolatry, strife, divisions, envy, or drunkenness you will not find healing, hope, peace or joy. Though these may seem to ease your pain temporarily, they will only prolong the pain of grief.

Now read Galatians 5:22-25 to the right and underline or lightly shade the fruit(s) of the spirit that promote healing.

GALATIANS 5:22-25

²² But the fruit of the Spirit is love, joy, peace, patience, kindness, goodness, faithfulness, ²³ gentleness, self-control; against such things there is no law. ²⁴ And those who belong to Christ Jesus have crucified the flesh with its passions and desires. ²⁵ If we live by the Spirit, let us also keep in step with the Spirit.

God does soften the blow of our loss over time. As we move further from our loved one's date of death and all that happened leading up to it we gain perspective. We notice that we're surviving. We see that the pain of loss is getting a bit easier to bear. But time itself does *not* heal wounds.

What does make the big difference is time spent seeking God, studying and applying His Holy Word, praying, and doing the next right thing will heal your wounded heart. How do you know what the next right thing is? How do we learn what God has for us to do and how to apply Scripture in our lives? By studying the Bible and seeking wise counsel from godly men and women!

Early in our grief, in the days following our loss, we do not need people rebuking us for wrong doctrine. We don't need to be corrected every time we say something that doesn't line up with the Scripture. We need help just getting through days of intense pain, decisions to be made, and the reality that we have lost someone we love. But a time comes when we need gentle reminders from God's Word. We need help getting back on the solid ground of God's Truth.

For us, as time passed and we sought the Lord we could look back to see the beautiful things God had done in the midst of our grief. In the time since The Accident we have seen young people change their behavior regarding alcohol and driving. We have seen many come to life in Christ. We have seen a friend's family restored after they realized their disagreements were petty compared to what could happen in an instant, compared to what it would be like to see their adult child die. We've seen our relationships with Christ move to a new, deeper level during the time since The Accident.

You may have had someone experienced with loss say to you, "You will never get over this. It never gets better. This pain is now your New Normal." Dear one, God promises in His Word that those who mourn will be comforted. For many the pain gets worse before it gets better, but it does get better if we ask God to work in our lives and emotions. If we seek God, study His Word, and apply it we grow in the fruit of the Spirit which includes peace and joy, and we learn to be led by the Holy Spirit and keep in step with Him. Yes, you will still think about your loss and still hurt over it sometimes. The person you loved still matters to you. But God is near the brokenhearted and He is our Healer.

Without studying the Word you will likely grow bitter and end up like the psalmist at one point:

PSALM 73:21-22

[21] *When my soul was embittered, when I was pricked in heart,* [22] *I was brutish and ignorant; I was like a beast toward you.*

But look at what God promises to those who seek Him through His Word. List key words that tell you how to do this and what you will receive from it.

PROVERBS 2:1-6

[1] *My son, if you receive my words and treasure up my commandments with you,* [2] *making your ear attentive to wisdom and inclining your heart to understanding;* [3] *yes, if you call out for insight and raise your voice for understanding,* [4] *if you seek it like silver and search for it as for hidden treasures,* [5] *then you will understand the fear of the LORD and find the knowledge of God.* [6] *For the LORD gives wisdom; from his mouth come knowledge and understanding.*

Just Journaling

Beloved, always begin your study of this book with prayer. Today, write a prayer asking God to show you His truth as you go through this book. Ask Him to reveal Himself to you.

As you go through this study you may want to highlight scriptures that touch you in a special way with a colored pen or pencil, or a box around them.

Answers to our questions are found in the Word. God has revealed in His Word what He wants us to know, what we need to know to be complete.

2 TIMOTHY 3:16-17

[16] *All Scripture is breathed out by God and profitable for teaching, for reproof, for correction, and for training in righteousness,* [17] *that the man of God may be complete, equipped for every good work.*

So let's look at what God says about why we should study the Bible during grief.

Read Psalm 119:24-32. Underline all references to *God's Word* and synonyms such as *testimonies, ways, statutes, precepts, works, law,* and *commandments.* Note what you learned about how studying God's Word can help you.

PSALM 119:24-32

²⁴ *Your testimonies are my delight; they are my counselors.* ²⁵ *My soul clings to the dust; give me life according to your word!* ²⁶ *When I told of my ways, you answered me; teach me your statutes!* ²⁷ *Make me understand the way of your precepts, and I will meditate on your wondrous works.* ²⁸ *My soul melts away for sorrow; strengthen me according to your word!* ²⁹ *Put false ways far from me and graciously teach me your law!* ³⁰ *I have chosen the way of faithfulness; I set your rules before me.* ³¹ *I cling to your testimonies, O LORD; let me not be put to shame!* ³² *I will run in the way of your commandments when you enlarge my heart.*

Read the statements below, which are common among grieving people. Highlight or underline any that are true for you. Then review Psalm 119:24-32 above to see if there are answers. If there are, list the verse number(s) to the right of each bullet.

- I'm hurting and confused; I need counsel.
- I feel like I'm dying inside, this hurts so much.
- I wonder if I could have prevented this. I don't understand God's ways.
- My soul is weary with sorrow; I am so tired and weak.
- I have heard many misconceptions and harmful ideas about death and God's nature. What is true and what is false?
- I want to be faithful in my Christian walk but don't know how to do that while grieving.
- I don't want to act shamefully while grieving.
- My heart is broken. I need help.

Do you feel taunted by the enemy regarding your loss? How can you answer intimidating suggestions according to these verses?

Are you willing to learn from God's Word? Do you believe the answers to your questions are found in the Bible?

What does the Word say about itself?

PSALM 119:41-42

[41] Let your steadfast love come to me, O Lord, your salvation according to your promise; [42] then shall I have an answer for him who taunts me, for I trust in your word.

HEBREWS 4:12

For the word of God is living and active, sharper than any two-edged sword, piercing to the division of soul and of spirit, of joints and of marrow, and discerning the thoughts and intentions of the heart."

Are you struggling with thoughts and intentions in your heart or with those of others? By studying the Word of God you can learn how to discern them with truth. The Holy Spirit is your guide; He will help you learn and understand how to find joy and peace even as you grieve the loss of those you love.

Studying the Scripture will help us know truth so we can have the right attitude—a right heart towards God and those around us. When we're grieving, wrong attitudes or ideas regarding God's nature and our relationship with Him can have grave consequences. They can increase our suffering and that of those around us. Even worse, if we have wrong ideas and bad attitudes we may resist the work God desires to do in our lives during our grief.

The Bible makes it clear that suffering is part of the Christian life and that God uses suffering to do a significant work in our lives. Beloved, will you resist the work the Lord is doing in your life or will you "cry aloud to Him for understanding" (Proverbs 2:3)? God's Word will help you understand His nature—something many of us have wrestled with in our bereavement.

Conventional wisdom from our friends even within the Church may not line up with the truth of God's Word. Pop culture, which can have a tremendous impact on our thinking, can't lead us to right understanding. We must each make our ears attentive to wisdom and incline our hearts to understanding.

"For freedom Christ has set us free" (Galatians 5:1). It is possible to be enslaved through misunderstanding God's nature, just as Paul warned the Galatians about enslavement through distorted versions of the gospel (Galatians 1:6-9). However, the truth will set us free (John 8:32). Your sanity, your very life, are at stake here.

This is why we must study God's Word as we grieve.

Psalm 119 is all about how wonderful God's Word is. The psalmist extols the greatness of the Scripture. This psalm is a wonderful place to start your study of God's Word![1]

Psalm 119:68 says, "You are good and do good; teach me your statutes." Do you believe that God is good and He does good? If so, do you want to learn his statutes? Are you willing to do some work to study and learn then apply what you learn?

If so, read the verses from Psalm 119 quoted here. Underline all references to God's Word and any synonyms such as *commands, testimonies, ways,* and *precepts*. Note what you learn about how studying God's Word can help you below each group.

PSALM 119: 76-77, 92-93, 105, 114, 116-117, 143-147, 153

[76] Let your steadfast love comfort me according to your promise to your servant.
[77] Let your mercy come to me, that I may live; for your law is my delight.

[92] If your law had not been my delight, I would have perished in my affliction. [93] I will never forget your precepts, for by them you have given me life.

[105] Your word is a lamp to my feet and a light to my path.

[114] You are my hiding place and my shield; I hope in your word.

---

[1] Precept Ministries International has published a wonderful inductive study of Psalm 119 *(Sweeter than Chocolate: Psalm 119)* written by Pam Gillaspie. Go to www.precept.org for more information.

116 Uphold me according to your promise, that I may live, and let me not be put to shame in my hope! 117 Hold me up, that I may be safe and have regard for your statutes continually!

143 Trouble and anguish have found me out, but your commandments are my delight. 144 Your testimonies are righteous forever; give me understanding that I may live. 145 With my whole heart I cry; answer me, O Lord! I will keep your statutes. 146 I call to you; save me, that I may observe your testimonies. 147 I rise before dawn and cry for help; I hope in your words.

153 Look on my affliction and deliver me, for I do not forget your law.

This is our prayer as we go through this study:

God,

We know You are good and You do good, but we don't understand all that has happened. We are grieving! Please teach us. May Your unfailing love be our comfort.

If Your Word is not our delight, we will perish in our affliction. Help us to never forget Your precepts for by them You have preserved our life. Your Word is a lamp to our feet and a light for our path. You are our hiding place and shield. Help us put our hope in Your Word. Uphold us according to Your promise, O God, that we may live, that we may be safe, and that we may have regard for Your statutes. Even in our suffering let Your commandments be our delight. Give us understanding of Your testimonies that we may live.

With our whole hearts may we cry out to You as we grieve and heal. Help us keep your statues; help us obey You and be doers of what we learn, not hearers only. As we rise up early in the morning and cry for help, cause us to hope in Your words.

Amen.

Just Journaling

What are you thinking or feeling today? What are you hoping to get out of this Bible study? After reading these passages from Psalm 119 write your prayer in your Healing in Grief Journal.

Willing to Work
by Ron Duncan

God is good
My son was killed in an accident.

How can these both be true?

I am finding that there are answers,
Truth that actually does set me free.
I must work through not only my pain
but also my misunderstandings about life in Christ.
I must be honest, open-minded, and willing,
Willing to work,
but looking to God as the Answerer.

When we lose a loved one,
we have to work through some tough questions.
Christians have been wrestling
with many of these questions for centuries.
While very personal, my pain is not unique.
What part of me recoils at that truth, and why?

We are not alone—Choose fellowship!

We need not start from scratch, trying to "reinvent the wheel" of theology
through our own grievous and broken thinking.

We have a proven source of truth: the Bible.
We have the "old books" of Christian thinkers
Based on Scripture, proved over time to be sound,
We have the experience of others walking this path.

LESSON 3

Do You Still Believe?

As for that in the good soil, they are those who, hearing the word, hold it fast in an honest and good heart, and bear fuit with patience (Luke 8:15).

[Kathleen] In the years before we lost our son, I experienced many losses and trials. Some I cannot share because they are not my stories to tell. My life was not easy, but God was with me through all my trials. He used them to help me mature and taught me to trust Him.

I almost lost my husband to a serious infection. I was afraid he would die. He spent months in and out of the hospital. We went through years of more surgeries, then crutches and a cane before he was able to walk normally again.

My mother, father, father-in-law, and mother-in law all passed away within a few years of each other. I loved them all. Each loss was painful in its unique way.

My oldest son did two tours in the Middle East with the US Marine Corps. During one of them his unit had the highest casualty rate of any Marine unit since World War II. As his mom, I was afraid for him.

We almost lost one of our other children to an illness the spring before The Accident. He spent days in an ICU and weeks in a hospital. I was afraid he would die.

After losing our parents in such a short time and all the other trials I had faced, I became fearful that one of my children or my husband would die. I was still grieving the loss of our parents. It did not show to the world, but I was secretly afraid.

Through studying the Bible and with prayer I finally came to believe that God is in control; that all the days of our lives are written in His book before one of them came to be; that He knows the time and the hour of our death; and that there was nothing I could do to prevent death at its appointed time. I also came to believe God is loving and full of compassion and mercy. I knew that He would help me through any trials I faced. I came to believe these things because I had studied His Word. I began to have a lasting peace once again. I reached this place through trials, prayer, study, and experiencing the love of God in very real ways. I was no longer afraid that I would lose another family member.

Then, early one Tuesday morning, the death of my child became my reality.

Within moments of finding out that our son Andrew was dead, God tapped me on the shoulder and asked, "You believed My Word to be true for your husband and children when you went to bed last night. This morning, in light of Andrew's death, do you still believe?"

My answer was, "YES! I still believe!"

I still believe that He is a good and beautiful God, slow to anger and abounding in love. He is compassionate and gracious. He works all things for our good. He has a plan for our lives. He is faithful and true. He is the Way, the Truth, and the Life.

Yes, I was hurting! My world had been shaken! I had lost a son! We had many decisions to make and things to do regarding a memorial service, what to do with his apartment and his things, plus legal issues from The Accident. I was in shock from the unexpected death of our healthy, beautiful son, but I knew that I was loved by the Creator of the Universe. I knew that He would care for me and that He is my refuge.

I am grateful that God took me through the earlier trials so that I had grown in faith and perseverance. I am grateful that a friend introduced me to inductive study so I could learn truth straight from God's Word even as I cared for my mother-in-law. I was hurting badly after caring for her for weeks, watching as she slowly died from cancer. I had been closer to her than I had been to my mother; her death was very hard for me. The truth I learned from God's Word helped me heal in my grief over her death.

I am glad I studied the Word intensely over the few years before we lost Andrew so I knew the truth about God! God looked upon my suffering and delivered me—helped me find healing, peace, and joy—because I had remembered His law (Psalm 119:153). I am grateful, too, that I have a relationship with my Father; I know Him. I don't just know about Him, I know Him and He knows me.

PSALM 119:53

[153] *Look on my affliction and deliver me, for I do not forget your law.*

I still do not understand all He is doing, but I know His nature. I know God. I know I can trust Him.

Do you trust Him?

In your grief, do you trust God? You may have lost someone you love very much! It hurts. It's hard to understand why some things happen. Why did you have to lose your mother or brother? Why do people get cancer or have bad things happen to them? Why do children die? Some of these questions don't have easy answers. But even when we don't have easy answers or answers at all, God is still faithful and worthy of our trust.

Beloved, do you trust Him even though you do not understand everything He is doing or why things happen? Do you know God's love?

Just Journaling

As you begin this lesson, take time to briefly answer two questions: Do you trust God even though you do not understand everything He is doing or why things happen? Do you know His love? Answer them briefly here and in the form of a prayer, poem, or drawing in your Journal.

In our grief it is natural to question why things happen. It is normal to have questions about why a particular thing happened to us. It is easy to forget the things we have learned about God and who He is when we are grieving unless we make a conscious choice to remember truth. In our pain we need reminders of what He has done for us and what He promises to do. We need to remind ourselves of the truth about God.

In the last lesson, we looked at some of the promises in the Bible regarding God's comfort. I knew God, so I could trust Him. It's hard to trust someone you don't know so in this lesson we're going to learn about God.

Who owns and rules over all?

Read the following passages. Draw a triangle over the words *God, Lord, Heavenly Father,* and all pronouns.

Write what you learn about **God.** These passages teach many of the truths that came to *Kathleen's* mind in the moments after learning of our son's death. They're also some of the passages we studied in the years before The Accident. They gave us strength and comfort as we faced the pain and sorrow of loss.

DEUTERONOMY 4:39

[39] *know therefore today, and lay it to your heart, that the LORD is God in heaven above and on the earth beneath; there is no other.*

PSALM 103:19

[19] *The LORD has established his throne in the heavens, and his kingdom rules over all.*

ACTS 17:24-25

[24] *The God who made the world and everything in it, being Lord of heaven and earth, does not live in temples made by man,* [25] *nor is he served by human hands, as though he needed anything, since he himself gives to all mankind life and breath and everything.*

Read the following verses; draw a triangle over the words *God, Lord, Heavenly Father* and all pronouns. Draw a squiggly line under *days* and *hours*. Write down what you learn about the number of our days. We will look at some of these more in-depth in another lesson.

Number of Our Days

PSALM 139:16

16 *Your eyes saw my unformed substance; in your book were written, every one of them, the days that were formed for me, when as yet there was none of them.*

PSALM 39:4

4 *"O Lord, make me know my end and what is the measure of my days; let me know how fleeting I am!*

Can you add a day to your life by worrying? Could you have added a day to your loved one's life by worrying?

MATTHEW 6:25-28

25 *"Therefore I tell you, do not be anxious about your life, what you will eat or what you will drink, nor about your body, what you will put on. Is not life more than food, and the body more than clothing?* 26 *Look at the birds of the air: they neither sow nor reap nor gather into barns, and yet your heavenly Father feeds them. Are you not of more value than they?* 27 *And which of you by being anxious can add a single hour to his span of life?* 28 *And why are you anxious about clothing?*

Do some of these truths bother you? Truth is not always easy or comfortable, *but discomfort does not change it.* If the Author of All Truth is our Lord, our only hope is to pursue Him and His Truth. He promises to guide us into all truth (John 16:13).

Just Journaling

In light of your loved one's death, how are you feeling about God ruling over all and numbering our days? What do you think about all of your days being written in God's book? Is this a comfort to you, or does it give you angst?

Remember your Journal is a place where you can be completely honest.

God's Nature

When we don't understand God's nature, we may not understand why He allows certain things to happen. As Ron and I learned more about God's nature, we realized that we don't have to understand the *why* of what He does; we can simply trust Him.

Let's look at some verses that address God's nature. These were precious to us as we walked through grief! Knowing God's nature helped us trust Him even when our emotions told us we were all alone and God didn't care.

Read the following verses and mark *God, Lord,* and synonyms that refer to Him with a triangle, then note what they say about Him.

PSALM 34:8

⁸ Oh, taste and see that the Lᴏʀᴅ is good! Blessed is the man who takes refuge in him!

PSALM 103:8-10

⁸ The Lᴏʀᴅ is merciful and gracious, slow to anger and abounding in steadfast love. ⁹ He will not always chide, nor will he keep his anger forever. ¹⁰ He does not deal with us according to our sins, nor repay us according to our iniquities.

ROMANS 8:28

⁸ And we know that for those who love God all things work together for good, for those who are called according to his purpose.

DEUTERONOMY 7:9

*⁹ Know therefore that the L*ORD *your God is God, the faithful God who keeps covenant and steadfast love with those who love him and keep his commandments, to a thousand generations*

1 CORINTHIANS 1:9

⁹God is faithful, by whom you were called into the fellowship of his Son, Jesus Christ our Lord.

JOHN 14:6

⁶Jesus said to him, "I am the way, and the truth, and the life."

PSALM 147:1-3

*¹ Praise the L*ORD*! For it is good to sing praises to our God; for it is pleasant, and a song of praise is fitting. ² The* L*ORD builds up Jerusalem; he gathers the outcasts of Israel. ³ He heals the brokenhearted and binds up their wounds.*

One last Scripture—Read Psalm 116:15. Note what it says about the death of a saint.

PSALM 116:15

¹⁵ Precious in the sight of the Lord is the death of his saints.

Summarize what you learned about God's sovereignty—what He owns and what He rules over—from this lesson. What do you remember about His nature, what He has done, and what He promised to do?.

Isn't it comforting to know that God knows and loves us before we live out the number of our days? For us, knowing that God loved our son and was not taken by surprise by his death helped us. It made us feel more secure in Him.

For some, however, the idea that God knew about their loved one's death or somehow authorized it seems wrong. In their minds the idea that all our days are written in His book make Him appear to be mean. If you feel this way, please continue with this study! It is important that you understand God's nature.

It is hard to lose a parent, spouse, child, sibling, or friend. We grieve and feel pain over our loss. We do not understand everything that happens, but we can understand from Scripture that *God is love*. He loves us. He cares for us. Yes, He numbers our days and knows each of them before one of them comes to be; and yes, we'll say it again: He loves us!

We do not understand how it all works, but we do know that God loves us, loves our family, and loves our son. He knew about liver disease, heart disease, cancer, and The Accident before they happened. We trust Him because we have a relationship with Him, and we know His nature. Though we may not understand all He does, the truth is that God is love. All He does . . . flows from His love.

Read 1 John 4:7-10. Mark the words *God* and *love*.

Where does love come from?

According to this passage, who has been born of God? Who knows God?

According to verse 8, who does not know God? Why?

How was God's love made apparent?

According to verse 10, why did God send His Son?

1 JOHN 4:7-10

[7] *Beloved, let us love one another, for love is from God, and whoever loves has been born of God and knows God. [8] Anyone who does not love does not know God, because God is love. [9] In this the love of God was made manifest among us, that God sent his only Son into the world, so that we might live through him. [10] In this is love, not that we have loved God but that he loved us and sent his Son to be the propitiation for our sins.*

Propitiation means satisfaction, like a debt paid in full. Jesus paid the debt for our sins. Because of His great love for us God sent His Son to die on a cross for our sins. He died for our sins, was buried, and rose on the third day that we might live through Him. Because of what Jesus did, we can have a beautiful relationship with God!

Beloved, do you believe these things to be true? Even as you grieve the death of a loved one, do you *believe?* If not, ask God to reveal Himself to you. Ask Him to show you His love.

Just Journaling

We have looked at many verses in this lesson about God. In your Journal add to your "What I Learned About God" list. Write in your Journal any questions you still have about God and be willing to have the Holy Spirit show you. You may want to write out a prayer. Ask Him to reveal Himself to you.

Treasure in Jars of Clay
by Ron Duncan

If you accept the biblical perspective,
If you are honest, open-minded, and willing,
Suffering has the potential for priceless value.

Don't get me wrong—
I'm tired of it;
I don't seek any more of it.
I miss my son.

"Death is swallowed up in victory"
Paul says (1 Corinthians 15:54)
It will lose its victory and sting (55)
Yes it will. But for now it truly stings.

Yet, God can work
through our suffering if we cooperate
"So that we may be mature and complete,
not lacking anything" (James 1:4)
"God . . . will Himself restore you, and make you
strong, firm, and steadfast" (1 Peter 5:6-10).
"Suffering produces perseverance . . . character . . .
hope that does not disappoint" (Romans 5:3)
This alone is awesome, isn't it?

What if God "works in all things,"
Even my painful loss,
Not only for MY good (Roman 8:28)
But also for even greater good for others?
Can my clay jar of grief (2 Corinthians 4:7-18)
carry a treasure of mercy and grace to someone else?

Certainly, we are
Pressed, but not crushed,
Perplexed, but not in despair,
Persecuted, but not abandoned
Struck down, but not destroyed.

We wear the death of our child
like a wet overcoat,
While Paul
"always carried around . . . the death of Jesus."
Can we, like Paul,
have the Life of Christ revealed in us
in the very heart of our grief and suffering?

Will we say, "we do not lose heart,"
Outwardly wasting away in grief,
Understanding that is temporary
Yet inwardly being renewed day by day,
Understanding this is eternal?

Will we see that our light and momentary troubles
Are achieving for us an eternal glory
That far outweighs them all?

Will we fix our eyes on what is unseen:
Immanuel, "God with us,
Ruler of the Kingdom of Heaven,
which is now among us?

Will this be our life,
While we are waiting?

LESSON 4

Is It Okay to Be Sad?

He was despised and rejected by men, a man of sorrows and acquainted with grief (Isaiah 53:3).

In Sunday school and other group Bible studies, many of us have read the verses "Rejoice in the Lord always; again I will say, rejoice" (Philippians 4:4) and "Count it all joy, my brothers, when you meet trials of various kinds" (James 1:2). You may have had a well-meaning friend quote one of these to you with respect to your grief. Your friend may also have tried to tell you that you shouldn't be sad because your loved one is "in a better place" and/or "they would not want you to be sad."

Do these verses mean it's wrong for us to be sad? Is it wrong for us to grieve and feel sorrow when a loved one dies? Is it wrong to cry, weep, or mourn? No, of course not!

> *[Kathleen] In the last chapter I shared that in the moments after finding out my son was dead I still believed that God was loving, kind, compassionate, and gracious. I was hurting. I was grieving. I was horribly sad. Yet I still believed in the resurrection power of Jesus Christ. I knew my son was alive in the presence of Christ and I hurt worse than I had ever hurt in my life. Although losing my parents and in-laws hurt, this loss hurt in my whole being. I mourned, sobbed, and wailed. My faith in God and hope in the resurrection power of Jesus did not take away the pain and sorrow of losing someone I love dearly.*

> *Many days I wanted to call my mother-in-law to talk with her about things happening in my life. I miss her to the point of tears some days.*

> *Very close to three years after the death of my son, I was traveling on the highway to Amarillo, Texas. We used to drive this road with my in-laws to see my husband's grandparents. It is the same road we drove to see our son when he lived in Canyon, Texas. My in-laws and my husband's grandparents have died. My son died. I started to feel the pain of grief as I drove that road. I began to cry and even had to pull over in a parking lot*

where I sobbed for a while. I cried out to God in my pain, and I thanked
Him for allowing me to have these wonderful people in my life as I sobbed.
I am glad to have known each of them. I still miss them all. I am sometimes
sad when I think about the void each left in my heart when they died.

When someone we care about dies, it's natural to grieve. The definition of grief in the Oxford Dictionary is a "deep sorrow, especially caused by someone's death." When a loved one dies, we feel a deep sorrow; we feel a sense of loss. In our grief, we hurt and cry. Before we can begin healing we need to accept that the pain is real. We need to feel that pain honestly and work through it. God knows and understands this. He knows we will mourn when a loved one dies, and He promises to comfort us when we do.

MATTHEW 5:4

> *4 Blessed are those who mourn, for they shall be comforted.*

God is a loving and merciful God, full of compassion! He knows how it feels to lose someone you love to death. Note what Isaiah says about Jesus:

ISAIAH 53:3

> *He was despised and rejected by men; a man of sorrows, and acquainted with*
> *grief.*

To see this more clearly, look at how Jesus responded when one of His friends died. In John 11 we read the story of Lazarus. Jesus loved Lazarus and his sisters Mary and Martha. He had spent a great deal of time with them. Jesus knew He could (and would) raise Lazarus from the dead, yet he still wept.

In your Bible, read the story of Lazarus in John 11:1-44.

Now read verses 32-35 on this page. Draw a cross over *Jesus* and synonyms that refer to Him. Draw a teardrop over *weeping* and *wept*. Underline Jesus' response to Mary. Did He rebuke Mary for weeping?

Look closely at His reaction to Mary in verse 33. Did He tell her to "Get over it!" and "Be joyful!"?

What do you think the connection is between the last thing Mary said to Him (v. 32) and His internal response?

Why do you think that response was so great and what does this tell us about Jesus?

Now read Matthew 14:10-13. Draw a cross over *Jesus*.

JOHN 11:32-35

32 Now when Mary came to where Jesus was and saw him, she fell at his feet, saying to him, "Lord, if you had been here, my brother would not have died." 33 When Jesus saw her weeping, and the Jews who had come with her also weeping, he was deeply moved in his spirit and greatly troubled. 34 And he said, "Where have you laid him?" They said to him, "Lord, come and see." 35 Jesus wept.

MATTHEW 14:10-13

10 He sent and had John beheaded in the prison, 11 and his head was brought on a platter and given to the girl, and she brought it to her mother. 12 And his disciples came and took the body and buried it, and they went and told Jesus. 13 Now when Jesus heard this, he withdrew from there in a boat to a desolate place by himself.

John the Baptist was another friend of Jesus. They were also relatives who had known each other from the time John leaped in the womb when the two pregnant mothers (Mary and Elizabeth) convened. They cared for one another. John baptized Jesus. But King Herod later had John killed.

When Jesus heard of his friend's death, did He rejoice? According to verse 13, how did He react?

Do you sometimes want to be alone in your grief? Do you want to just get away from everyone around you? Do you think Jesus understands this? Based on these passages do you believe God understands that you are sometimes so sad about the death of your loved one that you want to isolate yourself?

Just Journaling

When you read about Jesus' response to the deaths of His friends, how do you feel? Do you like be to alone or with others? Write what helps you when you are sad.

Read Hebrews 4:15. The high priest in the verse is Jesus. Mark *high priest* with a cross and note what it says about Jesus.

HEBREWS 4:15.

[15] *For we do not have a high priest who is unable to sympathize with our weaknesses, but one who in every respect has been tempted as we are, yet without sin.*

Look back at Isaiah 53:3 on page 34. What do you learn about Jesus from that verse?

Does He understand our sorrow and our weakness?

One more question about Jesus' grief: What does His grief tell you about your own? Friend, think about this for just a moment: Was Jesus' grief sin? Read Hebrews 4:15 again and shade the word *sin.* Jesus learned that His friends had died and He wept . . . but did He sin? No, Jesus was without sin. Sadness, sorrow, and tears do not mean we have lost hope or have no confidence in the resurrection power of Jesus. Many things that happen in this world are worthy of sadness. The death of someone we love is one of the worst; it is very worthy of sadness.

What does this tell you about your own grief?

There are many examples in Scripture of how God's people responded to the death of love ones. We will look at a few of them. Read the verses. Draw a teardrop over the words *mourn/mourned, lamented,* and *weep/wept* and a tombstone over the words *dead, perished* and *fallen by the sword.* Note what you learn about **Who** is grieving, **Who** they are grieving **for,** and **How** they grieve.

Who's grieving?

For whom?

GENESIS 23:2

²*And Sarah died at Kiriath-arba (that is, Hebron) in the land of Canaan, and Abraham went in to mourn for Sarah and to weep for her.*

How?

This passage is part of the story of Joseph, son of Jacob, grandson of Isaac, and great-grandson of Abraham. Joseph's brothers did not like Joseph. They threw him into a pit while deciding what they should do with him. Their jealousy had motivated them to get rid of him. Rather than kill him, they sold him into slavery and then took his coat, dipped it in goat's blood, and showed it to their father, Jacob, leading him to believe that he had been killed by wild animals.

Who's grieving?

For whom?

How?

Did Jacob's grief for his son last only a little while? How long did he say he would mourn?

GENESIS 37:32-35

32 And they sent the robe of many colors and brought it to their father and said, "This we have found; please identify whether it is your son's robe or not." 33 And he identified it and said, "It is my son's robe. A fierce animal has devoured him. Joseph is without doubt torn to pieces." 34 Then Jacob tore his garments and put sackcloth on his loins and mourned for his son many days. 35 All his sons and all his daughters rose up to comfort him, but he refused to be comforted and said, "No, I shall go down to Sheol to my son, mourning." Thus his father wept for him.

We know from the rest of the story that Joseph was not dead, but Jacob responded according to the news that he had been violently killed.

If you have time to read the rest of the story of Joseph, do so! It is a wonderful story of how God can use for good what the enemy plans for evil. In the end, Jacob is reunited with his son Joseph in Egypt! They had a beautiful reunion.

Just as Jacob was reunited with his son, we will one day be reunited with our son!

Do you realize that if you are a believer you will be reunited with other believers some day? For Christians, this is good news! Our loved ones who followed Jesus are not "lost" even though their life on earth has ended! Those saints who died before you are in the presence of Christ right now. When you die, you will be united with them if you, too, are a Christian. Isn't that wonderful news? That is something to rejoice about!

Continue to note what you learn about who is grieving, who they are grieving for, and how they grieve.

Read Numbers 20:29.

Who's grieving?

For whom?

How?

NUMBERS 20:29

²⁹ *And when all the congregation saw that Aaron had perished, all the house of Israel wept for Aaron thirty days.*

Here, David has just learned of the death of King Saul and his friend Jonathan, the king's son.

Who's grieving?

For whom?

How?

2 SAMUEL 1:11-12, 17

¹¹ *Then David took hold of his clothes and tore them, and so did all the men who were with him.* ¹² *And they mourned and wept and fasted until evening for Saul and for Jonathan his son and for the people of the Lᴏʀᴅ and for the house of Israel, because they had fallen by the sword.*

¹⁷ *And David lamented with this lamentation over Saul and Jonathan his son,*

During his son's illness, David fasted and prayed but the child soon died.

Who's grieving?

For whom?

How?

2 SAMUEL 12:19-20

[19] *But when David saw that his servants were whispering together, David understood that the child was dead. And David said to his servants, "Is the child dead?" They said, "He is dead."* [20] *Then David arose from the earth and washed and anointed himself and changed his clothes. And he went into the house of the LORD and worshiped.*

For many families, grief begins when they receive the diagnosis from the doctors. They learn that the illness is terminal; they find out their family member will die. They grieve through the time spent caring for their loved one.

After their loved one passes, their grief may seem to last only a short time. But this does *not* mean they didn't love their family member or friend who died, nor does it mean they stopped grieving. It simply means their grief has become more internal.

> *[Kathleen] My mother-in-law died after a battle with pancreatic cancer. Rita was a beautiful woman who had suffered from cancer for many months. In her last few weeks she was in great pain. It was a blessing for her when her body finally died. She had been a follower of Christ since early childhood. She knew Him and she knew she would be going into His presence when she died. We were sad that Rita was no longer physically in our lives here on earth but glad she no longer suffered. Yes, I grieved during the weeks I cared for her in her home. Those weeks were very hard! I cried often, usually in my room at night after she'd gone to sleep. Yes, I miss having her in my daily life. But I am grateful she no longer suffers and that she is in the presence of Christ.*

Read Job 1:18-22, and 2:13.

What did Job do when he learned that his children had died?

List each statement he made.

What does the author conclude about him? Taking vv. 21 and 22 together, what is it possible to say about the Lord and still not sin?

How long did Job's friends remain silently with him? Do you think that was good or bad?

JOB 1:18-22

18 While he was yet speaking, there came another and said, "Your sons and daughters were eating and drinking wine in their oldest brother's house, 19 and behold, a great wind came across the wilderness and struck the four corners of the house, and it fell upon the young people, and they are dead, and I alone have escaped to tell you." 20 Then Job arose and tore his robe and shaved his head and fell on the ground and worshiped. 21 And he said, "Naked I came from my mother's womb, and naked shall I return. The LORD gave, and the LORD has taken away; blessed be the name of the LORD." 22 In all this Job did not sin or charge God with wrong.

JOB 2:13

13 And they sat with him on the ground seven days and seven nights, and no one spoke a word to him, for they saw that his suffering was very great.

Chapter 3 records Job's lament. He cries out to God and tells of his pain and struggles. If you have time, read his lament in your Bible and write out what you learn.

Job was honest with God about his grief, yet he "did not sin or charge God with wrong."

Just Journaling

Do you have some of the same thoughts and feelings Job expressed? Write in your Journal how you feel. Draw a picture or write a poem.

How Did People in Biblical Times Grieve?

Let's look at one last example of how people in the Bible responded to the death of someone they loved. Read Acts 8:2. Stephen was a leader in the church in Jerusalem. He was stoned to death by a crowd. Let's see how some believers responded.

ACTS 8:2

> [2] *Devout men buried Stephen and made great lamentation over him.*

In all the passages we've surveyed we've seen that godly men and women in biblical times grieved and mourned. They were sad and they wept. Their grief was not expressed the same way; each grieved in unique ways. Jesus went to a desolate place; Job had friends around him in his suffering though they aggravated him more than anything; Jacob said he would grieve his son until he died while David got up, changed clothes, and went to the house of the Lord when Bathsheba's child died.

It is okay to be sad, to weep, to mourn, and to grieve when someone we love dies. It's okay to grieve your way. It is also important to not sin in our grief. Jesus did not sin though He was troubled after the deaths of His friends and He wept. Job lost ten children in one event, yet he too did not sin in his grief.

Friend, it is also okay to feel joy and laugh. We've heard from many that they felt guilty when they were happy and even laughed soon after losing a loved one. When Kathleen's dad died, we told many stories from our fond memories of being with him. Friends of his came to the house and shared their stories. He was a wonderful man and we loved hearing those stories. They made us happy even as we mourned his death.

As you study God's Word, setting your mind on things above, and begin to heal in your grief, you will find you have gained true perspective on life and the times of sadness and sorrow will become fewer and farther between. Times of joy and peace will become the norm. For some this happens more quickly than for others. Please know that it is a good thing to begin to feel joy and peace; after all, they *are* part of the fruit of the Spirit. This does not mean you have forgotten your loved one or, as some say, that you are "betraying their memory."

As a friend of ours wrote,

> I was thinking over Philippians 3:1 the other day: "Finally, my brothers, rejoice in the Lord. To write the same things again is no trouble to me, and it is a safeguard for you."

> Wondering why it is a safeguard? I think because when we set our minds on the Lord it's really difficult to set them on other things, like feeling sorry for ourselves, or being jealous of others, or whatever. Having joy in the Lord safeguards our minds from sin! We see this in the Psalms where David works through his fear, grief, or mourning by rejoicing and setting his mind on the Lord's Word to gain a right perspective on life.

Feelings in themselves are generally neither good nor bad; they're simply part of being human. Today you may feel sad or happy. These feelings are neither sinful nor righteous, however, they can progress to wrong (selfish) attitudes and actions. To avoid this the Christian must choose to set his mind on things above. We don't have to be driven by our feelings; we can be driven by the Word of God. Look at what Paul says:

COLOSSIANS 3:1-3

> [1] If then you have been raised with Christ, seek the things that are above, where Christ is, seated at the right hand of God. [2] Set your minds on things that are above, not on things that are on earth. [3] For you have died, and your life is hidden with Christ in God.

We must set our minds on things that are above, that is, God's perspective and values on our current situation. The Word judges the thoughts and attitudes of the heart (Hebrews 4:12), helping us identify and turn from the works of the flesh listed in Galatians 5:20: idolatry, sorcery, enmity, strife, jealousy, fits of anger, rivalries, dissensions, and divisions.

Paul says "If we live by the Spirit, let us also keep in step with the Spirit (Galatians 5:25). Some of our greatest yet unnecessary burdens in grief are rooted in selfishness. Our loving Lord will deliver us from this if we are willing to let His Word judge our thoughts and attitudes. He will help us keep from sin as we grieve.

We saw that both David and Job lamented to God about their losses. A lament is a passionate expression of grief and sorrow. One way to keep from sinning in our grief is to honestly express our pain and sorrow to God in prayer or song. Many times in the Psalms we see David pour out his heart to God. He expresses his grief and pain honestly, but he almost invariably ends with praise. David knew that even in sorrow and pain God is worthy of praise.

Read the following passages from the Psalms. Notice what David says about sorrow, grief, and death. Mark *sorrow, weeping,* and *death* with a teardrop. Put a tombstone through the word *death*. Then note how he ends each psalm. Underline the psalmist's conclusion (the first one is done for you). Write down what you learn about how the psalmist responds to sorrow, fear, and attacks. This may seem tedious, but writing it out will help you understand and recall truth.

Responses To Sorrow

PSALM 13:1-2, 5-6

[1] How long, O Lord? Will you forget me forever? How long will you hide your face from me? [2] How long must I take counsel in my soul and have sorrow in my heart all the day?

[5] But I have trusted in your steadfast love; my heart shall rejoice in your salvation. [6] I will sing to the Lord, because he has dealt bountifully with me.

PSALM 23:4, 6

[4] Even though I walk through the valley of the shadow of death, I will fear no evil, for you are with me; your rod and your staff, they comfort me.

[6] Surely goodness and mercy shall follow me all the days of my life, and I shall dwell in the house of the LORD forever.

Responses To Sorrow

PSALM 30:5, 11-12

⁵ For his anger is but for a moment, and his favor is for a lifetime. Weeping may tarry for the night, but joy comes with the morning.

¹¹ You have turned for me my mourning into dancing; you have loosed my sackcloth and clothed me with gladness,

¹² that my glory may sing your praise and not be silent. O Lord my God, I will give thanks to you forever!

PSALM 56:1-3

¹ Be gracious to me, O God, for man tramples on me; all day long an attacker oppresses me; ² my enemies trample on me all day long, for many attack me proudly. ³ When I am afraid, I put my trust in you.

Just Journaling

In the Psalms you just studied we hope you noticed that the Psalmist always comes back to trusting and praising God. Add to your list of "What I Learned About God" in your Journal. Write down how you have responded to sorrow, fear, and grief. Is this how you want to respond? If not, talk to God and ask Him to change the way you're responding to suffering.

Going from Weeping to Joy

We are part of an online grief support group. When a friend posted a comment about her misery in grief and how she thought she would always hate Saturdays because that's the day her daughter died, Lois, a mom who also lost her daughter, wrote,

Caroline just turned 20 and went Home in a car accident. I felt the same way as you at 10 weeks and at 12 months. On the first anniversary of her death I went into the bathroom, locked the door, turned on the water and

said "God, I will hate this day for the rest of my life. I will hate, hate, hate it!"

But His sweet gentle Spirit said to me, "This is the day which the Lord hath made, I will rejoice and be glad in it." I fell to my knees and wept: "God you will have to teach me how to rejoice on this day of all days."

He has. Every morning for the last 17 years and 11 months when I first woke up, my first thought was that verse.

It hurts to breathe, I know. Immerse yourself in His Word, daily, constantly. He will carry you.

Much love to you.

How do we go from weeping to being joyful again? How do we go from mourning to dancing? Lois's story tells us the first steps of healing in grief: Cry out to God honestly; ask the Holy Spirit to speak to you as you study the Bible; act on what He shows you in His Word.

Healing in grief takes time and work. Learning to find joy and healing will take time—time spent in His Word, time spent in prayer and worship, time spent doing the next right thing, and time spent grieving. But if we seek the Lord and do what He tells us to do we will find joy and healing with the help of His Holy Spirit.

We will study more about how to find joy and healing in Christ as we go through the rest of this study. Let's start with looking at who bore our grief.

What are two results of Jesus' suffering on the cross? Underline them in this passage and then write them below it.

ISAIAH 53:4-5

[4] Surely he has borne our griefs and carried our sorrows; yet we esteemed him stricken, smitten by God, and afflicted. [5] But he was pierced for our transgressions; he was crushed for our iniquities; upon him was the chastisement that brought us peace, and with his wounds we are healed.

In Luke 4 we are told that Jesus went into a synagogue and read from Isaiah 61. After reading from the prophet He said, "Today this Scripture has been fulfilled in your hearing" (Luke 4:21).

Read Isaiah 61:1-3. Mark *me* with a cross. Draw a triangle over the words *God, Lord,* and *he.*

What did God annoint/send Jesus to do?

What will Jesus give us to replace our mourning?

ISAIAH 61:1-3

[1] *The Spirit of the Lord God is upon me, because the Lord has anointed me to bring good news to the poor: he has sent me to bind up the brokenhearted, to proclaim liberty to the captives, and the opening of the prison to those who are bound;* [2] *to proclaim the year of the Lord's favor, and the day of vengeance of our God; to comfort all who mourn;* [3] *to grant to those who mourn in Zion— to give them a beautiful headdress instead of ashes, the oil of gladness instead of mourning, the garment of praise instead of a faint spirit; that they may be called oaks of righteousness, the planting of the Lord, that he may be glorified.*

Summarize what you learned about sadness, grief, and mourning from these verses.

If you are hurting today, if you are grieving today, pray; express your sorrow and pain; pour out your heart to Our Heavenly Father who loves you with an everlasting love. He cares for you. He wants to heal your broken heart and help you find joy and peace. His peace is available to all who seek Him.

Just Journaling

Write out your prayer. Pour out your heart to God who loves you.

How are you doing this week? What are you feeling? Does knowing God loves you help you in your grief? Write about this in your Journal.

LESSON 5

We Grieve Differently...Together

If one member suffers, all suffer together; . . . (1 Corinthians 12:26).

In the last lesson we saw that people in the Bible grieved in different ways. It's the same today. Often spouses grieve differently. Members of the same family may grieve in very different ways. How do we deal with others who grieve differently from us?

*[**Kathleen**] In those early days and weeks of my grief I talked about The Accident, our son's death, and my grief a lot. And I cried a lot. I would often want to talk about my grief and pain at the end of the day just before bedtime because it helped me sleep better to put my thoughts into words. Ron, however, rarely mentioned his own grief or what had happened.*

One night as we were heading to bed I said to my husband, "You don't mention Andrew or talk about the accident very much."

He answered sternly, "No. No, I don't. I don't want to talk about my son being dead. I don't want to talk about The Accident. I don't like thinking about any of it!" He paused and then sweetly added, "But I'm willing to listen any time you want to talk about it."

I was grateful for his answer. It helped me understand what he was thinking and feeling. And it showed his love for me. In return I learned to not talk about my grief so much. I learned to take my thoughts to God in prayer before talking to my husband. And many times the conversation with God was enough; I didn't have the need to express my pain to my husband after taking it to the Lord. I also found an on-line support group where I could post some of my thoughts, and I started Journaling.

The times I did talk to my husband I was more sensitive to him and his feelings. For example, I tried not to bring it up just before bed. I had noticed that, though it might help me sleep better, he had more trouble sleeping after we talked about Andrew or his death right before bed.

I also realized he was dealing with things I wasn't. Ron faced some hard stuff which I had not faced. He called our adult children living out of town the morning of The Accident to tell them their brother was dead. He saw Andrew's face where the truck hit him, I didn't. He cleaned out Andrew's apartment with our other three sons while the girls and I stayed home and worked on gathering pictures and greeting visitors.

Sometimes our spouses and family members have images and thoughts they need to process before talking about their grief. Ron did. Patience and respect are required.

Over time we found a good balance. He started sharing his thoughts and feelings more while I talked and shared less. I listened more.

Now, three years later, we are able to talk freely about the whole thing though we rarely discuss The Accident details or the immediate aftermath. We laugh at stories from Andrew's life. We are sometimes sad together. Sometimes an advertisement or something we see online reminds us of the way life was when we had seven children at home, and we sit quietly together lost in our thoughts. We have learned that though we grieve differently, we can grieve together.

Just Journaling

Begin today by writing a prayer in your Healing in Grief Journal. Ask God to give you ears to hear and eyes to see what He wants to teach you in this lesson.

How should you handle others when they grieve differently?

First, read 2 Corinthians 1:3-4. Mark *comfort/comforts*.

According to these verses, who comforts us and when (how often)?

2 CORINTHIANS 1:3-4

3 Blessed be the God and Father of our Lord Jesus Christ, the Father of mercies and God of all comfort, 4 who comforts us in all our affliction, so that we may be able to comfort those who are in any affliction, with the comfort with which we ourselves are comforted by God.

Why does He do this?

What resource do we have to help others?

What can we do for our spouses or family members if they grieve differently from us? Read the following verses and note what you learn.

How should we treat those who are weaker than we are?

ROMANS 14:1

¹ As for the one who is weak in faith, welcome him, but not to quarrel over opinions.

ROMANS 15:1-2, 5-7

¹ We who are strong have an obligation to bear with the failings of the weak, and not to please ourselves. ² Let each of us please his neighbor for his good, to build him up.

Why should we do this according to verse 2?

⁵ May the God of endurance and encouragement grant you to live in such harmony with one another, in accord with Christ Jesus, ⁶ that together you may with one voice glorify the God and Father of our Lord Jesus Christ. ⁷ Therefore welcome one another as Christ has welcomed you, for the glory of God.

How should we live with one another and why?

Read the following verses and note what we are to do for the weak.

1 THESSALONIANS 5:14-15

> [14] *And we urge you, brothers, admonish the idle, encourage the fainthearted, help the weak, be patient with them all.* [15] *See that no one repays anyone evil for evil, but always seek to do good to one another and to everyone.*

Read the following verses and note what you learn about how to treat others.

PHILIPPIANS 2:1-4

> [1] *So if there is any encouragement in Christ, any comfort from love, any participation in the Spirit, any affection and sympathy,* [2] *complete my joy by being of the same mind, having the same love, being in full accord and of one mind.* [3] *Do nothing from selfish ambition or conceit, but in humility count others more significant than yourselves.* [4] *Let each of you look not only to his own interests, but also to the interests of others.*

According to this passage, where does our encouragement come from?

Even in the midst of the pain of grief, can you treat others the way Christ has treated you? Who helps us comfort others and be gentle and kind to those around us who are grieving?

Who are we to love and treat well according to Jesus?

LUKE 6:31-33, 36

> [31] *And as you wish that others would do to you, do so to them.* [32] *"If you love those who love you, what benefit is that to you? For even sinners love those who love them.* [33] *And if you do good to those who do good to you, what benefit is that to you? For even sinners do the same*

> [36] *Be merciful, even as your Father is merciful.*

From the passages you've read in this section, summarize what you have learned about how to treat others who are grieving even if they're grieving differently from you.

How are you doing in this area? While you grieve, have you found it difficult to treat others with kindness and compassion? Pray and ask the Holy Spirit to help you do this.

Just Journaling

Have you found it difficult to treat others with compassion and kindness during your grief? Write what you learned about your behavior as you studied this lesson. If you need to confess anything to God, do so. Write about it and ask God for forgiveness.

Should we judge *how* others grieve?

It's easy to judge how others are handling a particular situation, especially when we're handling it a different way. We may think people *should still be grieving* or that they *should be doing better* by a certain time. We sometimes don't like the way a family member expresses or doesn't express grief.

But is it our place to judge *how* another family member grieves? Do you want others judging the way you grieve? When we grieved, Ron and I said wrong things to each other and to others beyond our immediate family. We sinned. We were not always kind and compassionate. But we are so grateful that our family did not judge us but instead loved and forgave us. We tried to love one another and help each other as we grieved.

Let's see what the Scripture says about judging in general to consider how to apply it to our judging grief in other people.

You may not like the way other people are handling or expressing their grief. You may want them to do something differently. But is it your place to judge?

Read 1 Samuel 16:7. What does God look at? Can you see a man's heart?

1 SAMUEL 16:7

⁷ But the Lᴏʀᴅ said to Samuel, "Do not look on his appearance or on the height of his stature, because I have rejected him. For the Lᴏʀᴅ sees not as man sees: man looks on the outward appearance, but the Lᴏʀᴅ looks on the heart."

Note here what Jesus says about judging.

LUKE 6:36-38

³⁶ Be merciful, even as your Father is merciful. ³⁷ "Judge not, and you will not be judged; condemn not, and you will not be condemned; forgive, and you will be forgiven; ³⁸ give, and it will be given to you. Good measure, pressed down, shaken together, running over, will be put into your lap. For with the measure you use it will be measured back to you."

Write out what you learn about judging others here.

MATTHEW 7:1-5

¹ Judge not, that you be not judged. ² For with the judgment you pronounce you will be judged, and with the measure you use it will be measured to you. ³ Why do you see the speck that is in your brother's eye, but do not notice the log that is in your own eye? ⁴ Or how can you say to your brother, 'Let me take the speck out of your eye,' when there is the log in your own eye? ⁵ You hypocrite, first take the log out of your own eye, and then you will see clearly to take the speck out of your brother's eye.

Is it your place to determine how everyone else *should* grieve? Do you want others judging how you grieve or telling you that you should be handling your loss better than you are? If you do not want to be judged by others, do not judge them.

My friend, if you search the Scriptures you will *not* find a list of "Thou *shalt not* grieve this way"s or "Thou *shalt* grieve this way"s. There are no right or wrong ways to grieve. Grief itself is predominantly internal, a mental and emotional response to some horrific loss. As we saw in 1 Samuel 16:7, God looks at the heart but man looks at outward appearance. And as we saw in other passages, it is not our place to judge others.

It's one thing to not like the way someone is handling grief, pain, or sorrow; it's quite another to endure a family member sinning in their grief or personally attacking you or others because of it. They may even abuse themselves with drugs and/or alcohol to numb their pain. You may witness other self-destructive behaviors.

If you see a family member sinning in their grief, how should you handle it? How should you react when one of them hurts you or acts out in self-destructive ways in the midst of grief? Remember what you learned about how to treat others! *Even when we see our brother sinning we should still treat him as we would want him to treat us in identical circumstances. We are to be gentle and kind.*

Read the following passages and note what you learn about treating others.

How to Treat Others

GALATIANS 6:1
[1] Brothers, if anyone is caught in any transgression, you who are spiritual should restore him in a spirit of gentleness. Keep watch on yourself, lest you too be tempted.

TITUS 3:1-2
[1] Remind them to be submissive to rulers and authorities, to be obedient, to be ready for every good work, [2] to speak evil of no one, to avoid quarreling, to be gentle, and to show perfect courtesy toward all people.

How to Treat Others   **JAMES 5:19-20**

[19] My brothers, if anyone among you wanders from the truth and someone brings him back, [20] let him know that whoever brings back a sinner from his wandering will save his soul from death and will cover a multitude of sins.

Just Journaling

Is someone you care about in sin? As they grieve, are they lashing out or doing harm to themselves? Could you pray for them? Consider making a list of ways you can help them and gently restore them.

Compassion vs. Comparing

How should we treat someone who is grieving something other than the death of a loved one? Beloved, should we compare our loss of a loved one and our grief to the suffering of those around us? Or should we show them compassion regardless of the cause of their grief?

Do you feel more entitled to grieve the loss of your brother than your friend whose 10-year-old service dog died? Do you think your pain is worse than his? Do you know people who expressed grief for their pet, for their adult child who went off to college, for their marriage that ended in divorce? Do they need our love and compassion in their grief the same way we need their love and compassion in ours?

You may know someone who is grieving the loss of a job, a marriage, or a pet. You may hear parents talking about the grief they felt when their child moved away to college or married. They may even say things like, "This is the hardest thing in the world!" or "I don't know if I can stand this pain!" No, their grief is not the same as yours. There is no way to compare because there's no way to measure the pain of losing a loved one to death or the grief of having an adult child move across the country.

We who claim Christ should not try to compare levels of pain. We should, instead, do what Jesus told us to do:

JOHN 13:34-35

[34] *"A new commandment I give to you, that you love one another: just as I have loved you, you also are to love one another.* [35] *By this all people will know that you are my disciples, if you have love for one another."*

Now let's look at what the Lord *doesn't* want us to do. Read the following passages. Underline *judgment* and corresponding synonyms. Circle the words *classify* and *compare*. Note what you learn about comparisons, judging others.

Judging / Comparing

ROMANS 14:10-13

[10] *Why do you pass judgment on your brother? Or you, why do you despise your brother? For we will all stand before the judgment seat of God;* [11] *for it is written, "As I live, says the Lord, every knee shall bow to me, and every tongue shall confess to God."* [12] *So then each of us will give an account of himself to God.* [13] *Therefore let us not pass judgment on one another any longer, but rather decide never to put a stumbling block or hindrance in the way of a brother.*

2 CORINTHIANS 10:12

[12] *Not that we dare to classify or compare ourselves with some of those who are commending themselves. But when they measure themselves by one another and compare themselves with one another, they are without understanding.*

Judging / Comparing

GALATIANS 6:1-5

¹ Brothers, if anyone is caught in any transgression, you who are spiritual should restore him in a spirit of gentleness. Keep watch on yourself, lest you too be tempted. ² Bear one another's burdens, and so fulfill the law of Christ. ³ For if anyone thinks he is something, when he is nothing, he deceives himself. ⁴ But let each one test his own work, and then his reason to boast will be in himself alone and not in his neighbor. ⁵ For each will have to bear his own load.

Whose burdens does God's Word call us to bear?

If you think you are something when you are not, what are you actually doing?

So, friends, while we grieve and suffer, how are we to respond to others who are suffering? Let's consider two different approaches of relating to grieving people and their corresponding motivations: compassion and comparison.

When we show compassion we relate to others who are hurting: we identify and empathize with them; we even sympathize when we look for similarities. When they describe their situations we *recognize* them:—"I've felt like that" or "I thought like that"—although perhaps our circumstances were quite different. We understand they are hurting; out of compassion for them we "bear their burdens" by sharing similar experiences.

We may be reminded of our own situation and pain, but this should not be our focus except to heighten our awareness and understanding of their pain. Our pain helps us to be more compassionate because we know what it feels like to hurt. We also know what receiving compassion feels like. This is similar to our showing mercy when we understand we have received mercy, forgiving someone because we know we have been forgiven.

When we compare ourselves to others we tend to look for differences. We contrast our loss with theirs, asking ourselves whose loss was worse, more tragic, more painful. We speculate who was less innocent, less moral, less exemplary. *Our* situation is the primary focus while the other person's loss fades to the background. We in effect compare our feelings and pain to their external circumstances, our "insides" to their "outsides"—not a very just comparison at all.

Comparing easily degrades to competitiveness, rooted as it is in self-centeredness and pride. Pride is essentially competitive, its very nature. When people are proud of being tall and beautiful, they are actually proud of being taller and more beautiful *than someone else.* We recognize these examples of pride in others. What's harder to see is how equally pointless and wrong it is to compare our loss to that of another person this way. There literally *is* no basis for comparison, so why invent one?

Self-centeredness and pride often breed resentment and bitterness. How can we heal when our hearts are seething with anger at one whose grief we consider inferior to our own? This is contrary to the Christian's life in the Spirit:

GALATIANS 5:22-23

> [22] *But the fruit of the Spirit is love, joy, peace, patience, kindness, goodness, faithfulness,* [23] *gentleness, self-control; against such things there is no law.*

We must guard against bitterness, jealousy, and pride if we are to move forward into healing. We must keep short accounts. We must forgive fully and ask for forgiveness when we sin. Take *every* opportunity to love and shun a comparative, critical spirit!

As Christians we should not try to determine if others are worthy of our love and compassion based on the degree to which they suffer. It is not my place to judge if their pain is bad enough to warrant my compassion. I should rather:

ROMANS 12:15-16

> [15] *Rejoice with those who rejoice, weep with those who weep.* [16] *Live in harmony with one another. Do not be haughty, but associate with the lowly. Never be wise in your own sight.*

Keeping in mind:

GALATIANS 2:20

> [20] I have been crucified with Christ. It is no longer I who live, but Christ who lives in me. And the life I now live in the flesh I live by faith in the Son of God, who loved me and gave himself for me.

If we are believers, we have been crucified with Christ. We no longer live but Christ lives in us and we live a life of faith. We do as Christ did—He loved people; He cared for the poor, the sick, and the grieving without regard to His own needs or suffering.

Jesus Christ became sin so we could become the righteousness of God in Him (2 Corinthians 5:21). He redeemed us by becoming a curse for us (Galatians 3:13). He did not say that our lives, our pain, our suffering would be nothing compared to the torture and pain He went through when He was crucified. As He hung on the cross, Jesus Christ, the Son of God who knew no sin, did not say, "Father, they got themselves into this mess; their suffering is nothing like what I'm going through. They don't deserve My compassion and love." No! As He hung on the cross, Jesus cried out:

LUKE 23:34

> [34] . . . "Father, forgive them, for they know not what they do."

Our response to a suffering person should never be, "My pain is worse than yours. I'm grieving the loss of my parent/child/friend/sibling so I don't care that you're hurting. Your pain is not worth my compassion. Just get over it!"

As a follower of Jesus our response to any other hurting person should be, "How can I love you? How can I help carry your burden?"

As we begin to heal in our grief we are able to reach out to love and serve others in obedience to Christ. As we do this we begin to heal more in our grief. It is a beautiful cycle that continues in those we love and serve: as they heal, they are able to reach out to others who are hurting and that in turn helps their own healing in the process. It's a "lovely cycle" of increasing love and compassion for our fellow man.

Take Paul's urgent advice:

EPHESIANS 4:1-6

> *¹I therefore, a prisoner for the Lord, urge you to walk in a manner worthy of the calling to which you have been called, ² with all humility and gentleness, with patience, bearing with one another in love, ³ eager to maintain the unity of the Spirit in the bond of peace. ⁴ There is one body and one Spirit—just as you were called to the one hope that belongs to your call—⁵one Lord, one faith, one baptism, ⁶ one God and Father of all, who is over all and through all and in all.*

Now, my friend, how do you think you should react when family members grieve differently from you? What would it look like to help those around you who are hurting? Maybe you need to talk to God about this. Take time to confess to Him anything you need to confess and ask Him to help you love those around you who are also grieving. It may be helpful to write out your thoughts.

Just Journaling

I realized I had been judging the way my husband grieved. This was wrong. I confessed my sin to God and to him. We were able to grieve and heal together when I stopped comparing our griefs and negatively judging his.

In your Journal write about anything you need to confess. Ask God to forgive you. He promises that if we confess our sins, He is faithful and just to forgive us and cleanse us from all unrighteousness.

Then write out ways you think others could help you in your grief. This is a great tool for when someone says "If there is anything I can do to help . . . ." You will have a ready answer. Make a second list of ways you can help those around you who are also grieving. Try to do <u>one thing</u> for someone who is grieving this week, something as simple as a hug, a smile, or a prayer. Maybe you can write them a note of encouragement or get them a small gift to help them feel loved.

Bear one another's burdens!

LESSON 6

Why Do People Die?

For the wages of sin is death, but the free gift of God is eternal life in Christ Jesus our Lord (Romans 6:23).

After The Accident we had more than one well-meaning friend say things like "I guess God needed him in heaven more than you did" and "God needed another angel in heaven" and "I suppose he had to die so someone could get saved at the memorial service."

> *[Kathleen] One young woman asked me "Did Andrew die instantly or did he suffer?" I told her I didn't know and had no desire to read the autopsy report because it wouldn't help me. What I do know is that his body died in The Accident but his spirit lives on in the presence of Christ. I know he's at peace and full of joy, surrounded by others worshiping God in heaven. I know that if he did suffer, God, who is loving, kind, and full of mercy had reasons for it and He never left Andrew; He promised to always be with His children. I also talked with her about how she can know Christ as Andrew did. Then I found a safe place to cry.*

> *Others asked me why Andrew died. I told them, "He died because of physics. When a very large truck going very fast hits the side of a small car carrying fragile humans, people tend to die. In this case, five humans died and one was in the hospital for months. Our son was one of those who died."*

> *This was not the answer they were looking for; they wanted a more spiritual answer. Surely God had reasons for such a great guy to die so young! Surely there are greater purposes for his death!*

> *When we experience the loss of a loved one, we want to know WHY they died!*

> *Sometimes the cause of physical death is obvious and easy to accept. When our 100-year-old Grandmother Estes died we understood and accepted that it was her time to die; she had lived a long and full life. My mother was an alcoholic most of her adult life and she drank so much her liver failed.*

My father had a history of heart disease. My in-laws both died of cancer in their seventies. Though it was painful to lose my parents and in-laws and I grieved each one, they had all become believers and their deaths were easy for me accept. It was easy to understand the death of a Navy SEAL who died saving his unit; he made a choice to be a warrior and defend his country and unit. He is a hero.

But five beautiful young people in The Accident? My friend hit by a truck while out for a morning run down our street? A beautiful godly seventeen-year-old girl or a sweet five-year-old boy nicknamed "Button-nose" getting brain cancer? My sweet friend raising three amazing young men getting colon cancer in her late thirties? Friends who are overdosing after years of sobriety? A Marine who makes it home from war safely then takes his own life? Baby Daniel, perfectly formed and beautiful but who died in the womb? Two-year-old Reece who died in a freak accident in the middle of the night? These deaths are hard to understand and accept.

When an infant or young person dies, we have trouble understanding why—why the accidents, cancers, murders, or suicides happen. We rarely ask "why" when deaths like these touch another family but we often look for some reason why our young family member or friend died.

Though pop-culture and well-meaning friends may try to explain why your loved one died, it is impossible to truly understand why people die without understanding the truth of God's Word. So let's look at some common but inaccurate claims of why people die and then what the Bible says about it.

My friend, some passages we are going to look at are hard. Always begin your study with prayer, asking God to help you be willing to listen to and learn truth. Ask Him to show you His truth and His ways.

Did this happen because of my sin? Am I being punished for some sin?

The good news of the gospel is that if you are in Christ by faith you are not being paid back or punished for your sins. Isaiah tells us that Jesus "was crushed for our iniquities and the Lord has laid on Him the iniquity of us all" (Isaiah 53:6). Because He paid our debt we are not punished for our sins. All of your sins were paid for by Jesus on the cross! In Psalm 103 (which we'll study in a later lesson) God tells us that He does not deal with us according to our sins or repay us according to our iniquities. He has removed our transgressions from us as far as the east is from the west. Your loved one did not die as punishment for sin.

We still face consequences of our actions here on earth. When the young man got behind the wheel drunk, he and four friends, including our son, died. My mother's lifetime of excessive drinking led to liver failure. Even as Christians we have bad things happen to us when we make poor choices, but God is not punishing us for our sin.

ISAIAH 53:5-6

5 But he was pierced for our transgressions; he was crushed for our iniquities; upon him was the chastisement that brought us peace, and with his wounds we are healed. 6 All we like sheep have gone astray; we have turned—every one— to his own way; and the Lord has laid on him the iniquity of us all.

PSALM 103:10-12

10 He does not deal with us according to our sins, nor repay us according to our iniquities. 11 For as high as the heavens are above the earth, so great is his steadfast love toward those who fear him; 12 as far as the east is from the west, so far does he remove our transgressions from us.

Did my loved one die because God needed another angel?

We will study whether people become angels at death in a later lesson but we can preempt the answer here which is "No!" God did not take your loved one because He needed another angel in heaven. He created angels and if He wanted another one, He could speak it into being.

A related general question is: Do people die because God needs them in heaven more than we need them on earth?

Read these verses and note what you learn about God and what He needs.

PSALM 24:1-2

[1] *The earth is the LORD's and the fullness thereof, the world and those who dwell therein, [2] for he has founded it upon the seas and established it upon the rivers.*

ACTS 17:24-27

[24] *The God who made the world and everything in it, being Lord of heaven and earth, does not live in temples made by man, [25] nor is he served by human hands, as though he needed anything, since he himself gives to all mankind life and breath and everything. [26] And he made from one man every nation of mankind to live on all the face of the earth, having determined allotted periods and the boundaries of their dwelling place, [27] that they should seek God, and perhaps feel their way toward him and find him. Yet he is actually not far from each one of us.*

Carefully read verse 25 again. According to verse 25, what does God *need?*

Did He take your loved one because He *needed* them in heaven?

God created the entire world; He doesn't need anything. If He did, He wouldn't be God. If God needed anything, He would not be complete (independent). God is complete. He alone is God. He chose to create us in His image. He chose to create the world. He *wants* relationships with us but He does not *need* anything.

Do people die to "get someone saved"?

We don't have time or space to study this in depth here, but the answer is "No!"

God uses all kinds of things in our lives for His glory and our good. People may come to know Christ through our loved one's death, but the Bible makes it clear that only One saves people and He does it *only* through His death. Yes, God may *use* your loved one's death in beautiful ways! But Jesus was the only One who could die for sins because He was the only Spotless Lamb. He knew no sin and He became sin so that we could become the righteousness of God in Him.

God so loved the world that He became man to live among us, a man born of the Holy Spirit and without sin. Jesus went to the cross willingly and died for our sins (Luke 22:42). He redeemed us from the curse by becoming the curse for us. He was buried and rose on the third day so that we would have a relationship with the Father through Him and eternal life in Him.

Do those we love die because God causes evil?

Some people believe that their child or parent died because God causes evil. They believe that He is an angry God full of hate and that's why people die generally. "He is just playing with us like an evil emperor," they believe. Is this true?

Read these verses and note what you learn.

How does this verse describe everything God made?	**GENESIS 1:31** ³¹ *And God saw everything that he had made, and behold, it was very good. And there was evening and there was morning, the sixth day.*

Remember studying God's nature in an earlier lesson? We read John 3:16, 36 and Romans 5:8. Now read these passages again with Isaiah 55:8-9 and Romans 8:28-30. Mark all references to *God* including pronouns and note what they say about Him.

God

JOHN 3:16, 36

[16] "For God so loved the world, that he gave his only Son, that whoever believes in him should not perish but have eternal life.

[36] "He who believes in the Son has eternal life...."

ROMANS 5:8

[8] but God shows his love for us in that while we were still sinners, Christ died for us.

ISAIAH 55:8-9

[8] For my thoughts are not your thoughts, neither are your ways my ways, declares the Lord. [9] For as the heavens are higher than the earth, so are my ways higher than your ways and my thoughts than your thoughts.

ROMANS 8:28-30

[28] And we know that for those who love God all things work together for good, for those who are called according to his purpose. [29] For those whom he foreknew he also predestined to be conformed to the image of his Son, in order that he might be the firstborn among many brothers. [30] And those whom he predestined he also called, and those whom he called he also justified, and those whom he justified he also glorified.

God's nature is LOVE, not evil! He does not hate believers and cause them to die because He is angry. The Creator of the Universe, Our Heavenly Father, is Love. He loves us and wants a relationship with us!

Yes, God causes tragedies to work for His glory and for our good. We see examples of this all around us. But is our definition of "good" the same as His? Do we see things the way He does? In Isaiah 55 God says that we do not think like He thinks. We do not do things the way He does things. We are not God, He is. We must trust Him. Knowing that He is compassionate, gracious, slow to anger, full of mercy and abounding in love, we can trust Him to be a Good Father to us. We cannot understand all God is doing in our lives and in the lives around us, but we can know that He is good and is working in all things to conform us to the image of Christ.

Romans 8:28 says, "And we know that for those who love God all things work together for good, for those who are called according to his purpose." This does not mean all things that happen are good; we know some things that happen are horrible! It means that God will work all that we go through in our lives for our good. All of our experiences, suffering, joys, trials, and victories are being used to mold us, make us more like Christ and bring glory to Our Heavenly Father.

Just Journaling

Has anyone said one or more of these platitudes to you? —"I guess God needed him in heaven more than you did" and "God needed another angel in heaven" and "I suppose he had to die so someone could ge saved at the memorial service"? Did you believe any of them before this study? If so, write down the truth you have learned from God's Word. Remember, until we know something, we don't know it. The person who said one of these things to you may have been trying to help you.

Often, we who are hurting in our grief get angry with others when they say stupid or hurtful things. We will look at this more later, but today take time to forgive anyone who said something that hurt you. Bitterness does not help us heal in grief. Write down if you need to forgive someone today and do it today!

So why do people die?

The simple answer to this is that we live in a broken, fallen world and bad things happen, even to godly people. The more remote answer has to do with creation, a garden, sin, and the consequent condition of all men.

In Genesis 2 you will find the record of God's creation of man. Read Genesis 2:7-9 and note what you learn.

GENESIS 2:7-9

⁷ then the LORD GOD formed the man of dust from the ground and breathed into his nostrils the breath of life, and the man became a living creature. ⁸ And the LORD GOD planted a garden in Eden, in the east, and there he put the man whom he had formed. ⁹ And out of the ground the LORD GOD made to spring up every tree that is pleasant to the sight and good for food. The tree of life was in the midst of the garden, and the tree of the knowledge of good and evil.

Genesis 2:9 says the Lord planted a garden and placed man in it. He caused trees to grow. Two particular trees mentioned are the tree of life and the tree of the knowledge of good and evil. What did God say with respect to these two trees?

God's Words

GENESIS 2:16-17

¹⁶ And the LORD God commanded the man, saying, "You may surely eat of every tree of the garden, ¹⁷ but of the tree of the knowledge of good and evil you shall not eat, for in the day that you eat of it you shall surely die."

If you have time, read Genesis chapters 2 and 3. In chapter 3 you will learn that the serpent (Satan) spoke to Eve and convinced her to eat from the tree of the knowledge of good and evil. Then she gave the fruit to Adam (verses 1-7).

Read Genesis 3:17-19 and note what you learn. What was the result of Adam's disobedience to God's command?

Results of Disobedience

GENESIS 3:17-19

¹⁷ And to Adam he said, "Because you have listened to the voice of your wife and have eaten of the tree of which I commanded you, 'You shall not eat of

it,' cursed is the ground because of you; in pain you shall eat of it all the days of your life; ¹⁸ thorns and thistles it shall bring forth for you; and you shall eat the plants of the field. ¹⁹ By the sweat of your face you shall eat bread, till you return to the ground, for out of it you were taken; for you are dust, and to dust you shall return."

Because of their disobedience, their sin, man's body returned to dust and his soul departed and returned to God (Genesis 35:18; Ecclesiastes 12:5, 7). Verse 24 of Genesis 3 says that God sent man out from the garden and placed an angel with a flaming sword to guard the way to the tree of life. Genesis 5:5 says Adam lived 930 years and then died. The wages of sin was and is death.

Now read Romans 5:12.

How did sin and death come into the world?

ROMANS 5:12

¹² Therefore, just as sin came into the world through one man, and death through sin, and so death spread to all men because all sinned—

Who dies?

You may be asking, "Is that fair?" Adam and Eve messed up so we have to die? Is that the way this works?!" Read the following passages and mark *sin, sinned, die,* and *death*.

Sin and Death

ROMANS 3:10-12, 23

¹⁰ as it is written: "None is righteous, no, not one; ¹¹ no one understands; no one seeks for God. ¹² All have turned aside; together they have become worthless; no one does good, not even one."
²³ for all have sinned and fall short of the glory of God.

Sin and Death

Who is "the one who was to come?"

ROMANS 5:14

14 Yet death reigned from Adam to Moses, even over those whose sinning was not like the transgression of Adam, who was a type of the one who was to come.

ROMANS 6:23

23 For the wages of sin is death, but the free gift of God is eternal life in Christ Jesus our Lord.

HEBREWS 9:27

27 And just as it is appointed for man to die once, and after that comes judgment,

This is not to say that our loved one died at a specific time and way because of a particular sin or sins. That was the mistake Job's friends made, always intimidating him to "Fess up!" what he did that brought on his troubles. These are mysteries we don't and can't know because they're not revealed in the Word of God. We shouldn't speculate such things of ourselves and especially of others.

Just Journaling

Before you go on with this lesson, take time to think about what you just learned. How are you feeling about it? What questions do you still have?

Hebrews 9:27 says all of us are appointed to die once. According to Romans we have all sinned; that includes you and me. The wages of our sin is our death but the good news is we can have eternal life in Christ Jesus! It is the free gift of God.

Read Romans 5:12-14 and mark *sin* and *death*.

How did sin and death enter the world? List the events in order.

ROMANS 5:12-14

12 Therefore, just as sin entered the world through one man, and death through sin, and in this way death came to all men, because all sinned— 13 for before the law was given, sin was in the world. But sin is not taken into account when there is no law. 14 Nevertheless, death reigned from the time of Adam to the time of Moses, even over those who did not sin by breaking a command, as did Adam, who was a pattern of the one to come.

We read about the Fall of Man in Genesis 3. We have a vague understanding that this changed everything. But in Romans 5 Paul expands our understanding: "sin entered the world" and therefore "death reigned." It is only when this becomes personal that we begin to see with a little more clarity what this means. The vagueness becomes painfully clear. Yes, as we buried our parents and son, "death reigned" . . . for the moment.

We typically think of "sin" as behaviors—lying, cheating, harming others, etc.— but the more complete understanding is that sin is our *condition* (which of course results in corresponding attitudes and behaviors). This condition is our very nature. You may find it more helpful to think of it as brokenness or diseased or missing-the-mark, but we must understand that it is our inherent condition. We are powerless to correct it ourselves. It is the nature of our world *because* it is the nature of people. Without Christ, it is my nature and yours; we are "by nature children of wrath, like the rest of mankind" (Ephesians 2:3). What is actually remarkable is that we are typically unaware of this condition. Compared to many people in the world we have a relatively wonderful life . . . until some disaster strikes.

Of course, when we put our confidence in Christ we received a new nature. We "died to sin" (Romans 6:2) and we began to "walk in newness of life" (Romans 6:4). We were delivered from spiritual death but physical death remains. And that is why bad things happen, even to those who have entered the Kingdom of God.

The bottom line is that we die because we live in a world under the condition of sin, a world where death reigns. Sin and death are in this world.

The Bible says "all have sinned and fall short of the glory of God" (Romans 3:23). We live in a broken world, but the sting of death which is sin (1 Corinthians 15:56) has been removed by Jesus' redemption and resurrection. Our loved ones who believed in Christ, according to Jesus' own Word, have eternal life. They are in the presence of Christ even now. Eternal life is available to you as well, my friend. You, too, can become a child of God and have eternal life.

Read the following passages and note what you learn about salvation.

Salvation

JOHN 3:16-18, 36

[16] *"For God so loved the world, that he gave his only Son, that whoever believes in him should not perish but have eternal life. [17] For God did not send his Son into the world to condemn the world, but in order that the world might be saved through him. [18] Whoever believes in him is not condemned, but whoever does not believe is condemned already, because he has not believed in the name of the only Son of God.*

[36] *Whoever believes in the Son has eternal life; whoever does not obey the Son shall not see life, but the wrath of God remains on him.*

HEBREWS 2:9, 14-15

[9] *But we see him who for a little while was made lower than the angels, namely Jesus, crowned with glory and honor because of the suffering of death, so that by the grace of God he might taste death for everyone.*

Salvation

¹⁴ Since therefore the children share in flesh and blood, he himself likewise partook of the same things, that through death he might destroy the one who has the power of death, that is, the devil, ¹⁵ and deliver all those who through fear of death were subject to lifelong slavery.

1 CORINTHIANS 15:1-8

¹Now I would remind you, brothers, of the gospel I preached to you, which you received, in which you stand, ²and by which you are being saved, if you hold fast to the word I preached to you—unless you believed in vain. ³For I delivered to you as of first importance what I also received: that Christ died for our sins in accordance with the Scriptures, ⁴that he was buried, that he was raised on the third day in accordance with the Scriptures, ⁵and that he appeared to Cephas, then to the twelve. ⁶Then he appeared to more than five hundred brothers at one time, most of whom are still alive, though some have fallen asleep. ⁷Then he appeared to James, then to all the apostles. ⁸Last of all, as to one untimely born, he appeared also to me.

1 JOHN 2:2

²He is the propitiation for our sins, and not for ours only but also for the sins of the whole world.

If you are not a follower of Jesus, today that can change.

Jesus Christ is the Son of God. He came to the world, born of a virgin. He was crucified for our sin, died, was buried, and rose on the third day. This is the good news! To become a child of God, a disciple of Christ, you must believe the gospel is true. If you believe this today, talk with God about it. Open your heart to Him, beloved. He loves you and wants to have a relationship with you and give you peace.

Just Journaling

If you are already a believer, write about your faith. How has your faith impacted your grief? If you want to become a believer today, write about your desire to become a child of God. Confess anything you need to confess and ask God to save you from sin and death. He will.

You may want to learn more about having a relationship with God. Precept Ministries offers a 6-Week Bible Study titled *Having a Real Relationship with God*.[1] This study will help you learn to walk with God.

---

[1] Kay Arthur, *Having a Real Relationship With God* (Colorado Springs, CO: WaterBrook Press, 2001).

LESSON 7

But Why *This* Person *I* Love at *This* Time?

For everything there is a season, and a time for every matter under heaven: a time to be born, and a time to die; (Ecclesiastes 3:1-2a)

In the last lesson we looked at why people die and how we can have eternal life. But you may be saying, "I know we all die sometime, but why did *my* loved one die *now*? Why did my child die so young? Who decides when we die?"

The answers to these questions may be contrary to what you have always believed and been taught. But we are studying God's Word to learn truth, even if it's hard and opposed to popular opinion. Beloved, keep the nature of God before you as you study these passages. God is love. He is compassionate, gracious, and full of mercy. Some truth is hard, but this does not change God's nature.

Before we go on, let us pray for you.

Father,

Some of these truths are difficult. They go against what the world says and we tend to believe. Help us open our hearts, ears, and eyes to Your truth. Help us understand Your ways. Remind us of Your nature as we read and study these passages. Lead us into truth and heal our wounded hearts as we seek You.

In the Holy Name of Your Son Jesus Christ I pray.

Amen.

Let's look at what God's Word has to say. Read the following verses and mark key words, especially references to *God* and *death,* and note what you learn.

God and Death

JOB 14:5

⁵ *Since his days are determined, and the number of his months is with you, and you have appointed his limits that he cannot pass.*

God and Death

PSALM 139:15-16

15 My frame was not hidden from you, when I was being made in secret, intricately woven in the depths of the earth. 16 Your eyes saw my unformed substance; in your book were written, every one of them, the days that were formed for me, when as yet there was none of them.

ECCLESIASTES 3:1-2a

1 For everything there is a season, and a time for every matter under heaven: 2 a time to be born, and a time to die;

ECCLESIASTES 8:8

8 No man has power to retain the spirit, or power over the day of death.

PROVERBS 19:21

21 Many are the plans in the mind of a man, but it is the purpose of the LORD that will stand.

Who is like God?

ISAIAH 46:9-10

9 remember the former things of old: for I am God, and there is no other; I am God, and there is none like me, 10 declaring the end from the beginning and from ancient times things not yet done, saying, 'My counsel shall stand, and I will accomplish all my purpose,'

According to Proverbs and Isaiah, whose purpose stands above all others' plans (men and angels')?

God and Death

DEUTERONOMY 32:39

[39] "'See now that I, even I, am he, and there is no god beside me; I kill and I make alive; I wound and I heal; and there is none that can deliver out of my hand.'"

1 SAMUEL 2:6

[6] The LORD kills and brings to life; he brings down to Sheol and raises up.

Beloved, you have looked at several passages from the Old Testament. Now go back and review them and summarize what you learned about God. Add this to your list "What I Learned About God" in your *Journal.*

Did you know that the God of the Old Testament is the same as that of the New Testament? Let's look at a few passages from the New Testament. Continue to mark key words, especially references to *God* and *death,* and note what you learn.

Where does God live?

What does He give and to *whom?*

What did He make from one man, and for what ultimate purpose?

What do we have "in him"?

ACTS 17:24-28

[24] The God who made the world and everything in it, being Lord of heaven and earth, does not live in temples made by man, [25] nor is he served by human hands, as though he needed anything, since he himself gives to all mankind life and breath and everything. [26] And he made from one man every nation of mankind to live on all the face of the earth, having determined allotted periods and the boundaries of their dwelling place, [27] that they should seek God, in the hope that they might feel their way toward him and find him. Yet he is actually not far from each one of us, [28] for "In him we live and move and have our being."

Who holds the keys to death?

REVELATION 1:17-18

[17] *When I saw him, I fell at his feet as though dead. But he laid his right hand on me, saying, "Fear not, I am the first and the last,* [18] *and the living one. I died, and behold I am alive forevermore, and I have the keys of Death and Hades."*

Again, this may seem strange or different from what you've heard before but remember, we are studying God's Word to learn truth and apply it in our lives so that we can find peace and healing as we are conformed to the image of Christ. Beloved, according to these passages, who controls life and death?

Do you believe this? It is written in the Scriptures, scriptures inspired by God, truths. If you need to take a few minutes or even days to think about this, that's okay. Ask God to help you understand and believe the truth. Then go on with your study of His Word.

Just Journaling

Beloved, what are you thinking? How do you feel about God numbering our days? Does this make you uncomfortable or comfortable?

Be sure to add to your "What I Learned About God" list.

According to truth found in the Holy Word of God, the Lord has power over life and death. No one can prevent death as we just saw in Ecclesiastes 8:8. God determines the time of our death. Some die sooner than others and some very young but according to the Bible everyone lives the number of days God ordained for them. And if God ordained the number of their days, they're "complete" in His eyes.

Matthew 5:45 says God sends rain on the just and the unjust; He also makes His sun rise on the evil and on the good. My friend, bad things happen to all kinds of people. We suffer. People die. It hurts and we don't have to like it; in fact, we can *hate* death as the last enemy (1 Corinthians 15:26). But to have peace we must accept that God rules over all: life, death, time. For us, it's comforting to know that God controls life and death. You wouldn't want a weak god who doesn't rule over death, would you? How could he save us out of it and from it?

What kind of god do you want to serve? Does God's sovereignty give you any comfort? Take time to write your thoughts. Look back at the passages you studied in this lesson and the ones before it. If you're keeping a *Healing in Grief Journal,* look at the list of what you learned about God. Then add what you learned from this lesson.

Even if it makes you uncomfortable, please stay with this study. In God's Word is life! There is healing to be found by seeking God, studying His Word and applying it to our lives.

Can we know *why* they died? Do we have a right to question God?

Beloved, the book of Job starts out with God calling Satan into account for his wanderings and Satan insulting God—that His work of art serves Him only because He's blessed him in every way. God responds to Satan, "Very well, then, everything he has is in your power, but on the man himself do not lay a finger" (Job 1:12). Read about this in Job 1. All ten of Job's children die. Satan and his subordinates pull the triggers but God gives him authority just as a human king would give one of his subjects. God ultimately controls life and death.

After severe trials that tortured his very body, Job appeals to God (chapter 31). He asks why he has gone through so much suffering. God doesn't directly answer Job's questions, but He does have a lot to say. Read Job 38:1-7 and 40:1-9. Note what you learn. If you have time, read through chapters 38-39.

How does God respond to Job?

JOB 38:1-7

[1] *Then the* Lord *answered Job out of the whirlwind and said:* [2] *"Who is this that darkens counsel by words without knowledge?* [3] *Dress for action like a man; I will question you, and you make it known to me.* [4] *"Where were you when I laid the foundation of the earth?*

How does God respond to Job?

Tell me, if you have understanding.
⁵ Who determined its measurements—
surely you know! Or who stretched
the line upon it? ⁶ On what were its
bases sunk, or who laid its cornerstone,
⁷ when the morning stars sang together
and all the sons of God shouted for joy?

JOB 40:1-9

¹ And the LORD said to Job: ² "Shall a
faultfinder contend with the Almighty?
He who argues with God, let him
answer it." ³ Then Job answered the
LORD and said: ⁴ "Behold, I am of small
account; what shall I answer you? I lay
my hand on my mouth. ⁵ I have spoken
once, and I will not answer; twice, but I
will proceed no further." ⁶ Then the LORD
answered Job out of the whirlwind and
said: ⁷ "Dress for action like a man; I will
question you, and you make it known
to me. ⁸ Will you even put me in the
wrong? Will you condemn me that you
may be in the right? ⁹ Have you an arm
like God, and can you thunder with a
voice like his?"

In essence God says "Where were you when I made all this? Who are you to question Me?" In Job 40:1-9 the Lord tells Job he should not contend with the Almighty, not argue with Him. Job agrees: "Behold, I am of small account; what shall I answer you? I lay my hand on my mouth. I have spoken once, and I will not answer; twice, but I will proceed no further." In other words, *I was wrong! I messed up in questioning You! I won't do that again!*

We read about the Fall of Man in the previous lesson. We learned that the bottom line is that people die because we live in a world under the condition of sin; a world where death reigns. Sin and death are in this world. But under this overarching general principle, we don't know why some people die very young and others very old, why some babies get sick and die while others are miraculously healed from the same disease, why some are killed or seriously injured in war and others survive and prosper. We don't have answers to these questions here on earth. We won't get answers to all our "Why?"s in this life, not even from the Word; we just have to wait until we see the Lord.

What we do know, because He's revealed it, is God's nature: He is love. He is just, kind, full of mercy, omniscient, powerful, and compassionate. He is King of Kings, Lord of Lords, Creator, Redeemer, Healer, our ever present help in times of trouble. He is a Good Father! We can trust Him even when we don't understand why bad things happen.

Keeping in mind that God is love, read 1 Corinthians 13:4-13 and mark each mention of *love* and all pronouns with a heart.

What do you learn about love? Make a list of everything this passage says about it.

Since God is love, what does this passage teach you about Him?

Read verses 8-13 again. Underline the words *I* and *we*. List the qualities of love.

1 CORINTHIANS 13:4-13

⁴ Love is patient and kind; love does not envy or boast; it is not arrogant ⁵ or rude. It does not insist on its own way; it is not irritable or resentful; ⁶ it does not rejoice at wrongdoing, but rejoices with the truth. ⁷ Love bears all things, believes all things, hopes all things, endures all things. ⁸ Love never ends. As for prophecies, they will pass away; as for tongues, they will cease; as for knowledge, it will pass away. ⁹ For we know in part and we prophesy in part, ¹⁰ but when the perfect comes, the partial will pass away. ¹¹ When I was a child, I spoke like a child, I thought like a child, I reasoned like a child. When I became a man, I gave up childish ways. ¹² For now we see in a mirror dimly, but then face to face. Now I know in part; then I shall know fully, even as I have been fully known. ¹³ So now faith, hope, and love abide, these three; but the greatest of these is love.

Note that Paul says we know only in part now; we see in a mirror dimly. Someday, when Christ returns, we will see Him face to face and know fully as we have been fully known. For now we must be satisfied that faith, hope, and love abide and that love is the greatest.

We must trust God. His judgments are unsearchable and His ways are inscrutable. But we will glorify and enjoy Him forever.

ROMANS 11:33-36

> [33] Oh, the depth of the riches and wisdom and knowledge of God! How unsearchable are his judgments and how inscrutable his ways! [34] "For who has known the mind of the Lord, or who has been his counselor?" [35] "Or who has given a gift to him that he might be repaid?" [36] For from him and through him and to him are all things. To him be glory forever. Amen.

Is God loving and kind? Absolutely!

Does He heal and rescue some people while permitting others to die of horrible diseases and the actions of others? Yes, He does!

So, does He determine when we die? Yes!

You may be shouting, "But what about our choices? Do they matter?" Of course our choices matter and we will give account to God for everything we choose and do in our lives.

Read Ecclesiastes 12:13-14, Matthew 12:35-37, Romans 2:16, and 2 Corinthians 5:10. Note what will happen on the day of judgment.

ECCLESIASTES 12:13-14

> [13] The end of the matter; all has been heard. Fear God and keep his commandments, for this is the whole duty of man. [14] For God will bring every deed into judgment, with every secret thing, whether good or evil.

MATTHEW 12:35-37

> [35] The good person out of his good treasure brings forth good, and the evil person out of his evil treasure brings forth evil. [36] I tell you, on the day of judgment people will give account for every careless word they speak, [37] for by your words you will be justified, and by your words you will be condemned."

ROMANS 2:16

> [16] on that day when, according to my gospel, God judges the secrets of men by Christ Jesus.

2 CORINTHIANS 5:10

> [10] For we must all appear before the judgment seat of Christ, so that each one may receive what is due for what he has done in the body, whether good or evil.

We will all give an account someday.

"But wait!" you say; "Didn't you just say that God numbers our days?" Yes, we did, because God said it. And He said people will give an account on the day of judgment. God says all these things in His Holy Word.

God numbers our days and people can kill other people or themselves, but they will give an account to God for their actions. (In a later lesson we'll look at what we should do if someone else is to blame for the death of our loved one.)

We see in the Old Testament dozens of examples of men killing men in battle: "Saul has struck down his thousands, and David his ten thousands" (1 Samuel 18:70). Some murdered: Cain murdered Abel. Some committed suicide, notably King Saul and Judas, the betrayer of Christ.

So how does this work?

Is God sovereign? YES!

Do our choices matter? YES!

This is one of those tensions in the Bible we cannot fully understand, like Jesus being fully God and fully man or God being one and three. But we can trust God and wait patiently according to this truth: "The secret things belong to the LORD our God, but the things that are revealed belong to us and to our children forever, that we may do all the words of this law" (Deuteronomy 29:29). When eternity first lights on us we'll have an entirely different perspective on the worst life threw at us; and as the ages roll by with our loved ones restored to us, the old life will pale more and more in comparison.

Why does God heal some and let others die? Why did our son suffer severe trauma that resulted in his death while others have survived horrific accidents without so much as a scratch? Why did our dear friend's daughter live for a week after hitting a tree but then succumb to death? Why do some recover from cancer while others languish in pain for months and then die?

Again, these are mysteries that we will not understand in this life. But we do know that God loves people. We know He promises those who love Him eternal life. We know He is compassionate, just, gracious, and kind. We know He is God . . . and we are not.

How do we reconcile God's sovereignty with man's choices? Theoretically we may not be able to but what we can do *practically* is submit to God and His Word. Isn't submission the very heart and crux of living a life that pleases God? As the old hymn says, "Trust and obey, for there's no other way, to be happy in Jesus, but to trust and obey." We trust what He says in His Word and live our lives accordingly, even when we don't understand it all.

A woman recently wrote to Kathleen and asked, "Why? Why did my 21-year-old son die? Is it because God thinks I'm strong enough to handle it? Is He disciplining my lack of faith or testing my strong faith? Is it because He wants more glory or needs my son? Do I have a supernatural bullseye on my back? Does God get pleasure out of my suffering? Why do we have to suffer?"

Before you read our answer, how would you answer her questions? Based on what you've studied in this lesson, what do you believe about *why* your loved one died? Do you think there's only one reason . . . or many?

Just Journaling

Based on what you've studied in this lesson, what do you believe about the reasons your loved one died? Do you find comfort in knowing God is sovereign? Write out your thoughts, questions, and feelings. Maybe write a poem or draw a picture.

Here is Kathleen's answer to the woman who wrote:

I am sorry. I'm sorry for your pain! I am sorry your son died.

No! God does not take our kids because we are strong enough to handle it! No, it's not because of your faith that your son died. Nor because of your lack of faith. No, you don't have a supernatural bullseye on your back God is shooting at.

When sin came into the world, according to Genesis, the Tree of Life in the garden was no longer available for us to eat from. God saw that man had eaten from the Tree of the Knowledge of Good and Evil and made man leave the garden. He disobeyed. He sinned. Because of man's disobedience (sin) the Tree of Life was no longer available to him. Death entered the world. That's why our kids, our parents, siblings, friends, and others all die, some sooner than others.

So, no, I don't believe that our sons are dead because we are weak or strong.

I do believe God uses ugly things in my life just as He uses everything—to work out His purposes. He uses ugly things like a violent sexual assault at age 18, my parents' divorce, addiction in those I love, mental illness in people I care about, job losses, financial difficulties, and even the deaths of my parents, friends, and my son. He uses ugly things to conform me to the beautiful image of Christ because He loves me. He can and does work in all things for my good because I love Him and am called according to His purpose. And just as God is ultimately good, His purposes for me are ultimately good.

People make choices. I do believe He knew about each of them before-hand. I do believe He never left me. I do believe His promises are true.

And because of His great love for us, He sent Jesus to become sin for us that we might become the righteousness of God and one day eat from the Tree of Life in the New Heavens and New Earth. Jesus came, lived as man, died, was buried, and rose again to give us eternal life the moment we believe.

I do believe that because of who He is, I will praise Him. I want to live a life that gives Him glory, not because my son is dead but because God alone is worthy of glory and honor and majesty. He alone is faithful, true, and just. He alone is good. He is love. And because of who God is, I will praise Him in the storm. I will live a life that glorifies Him the best I am able. I will trust Him and love Him, even in the midst of my pain.

Just Journaling

This may seem like a strange Journaling assignment, but it will help you as you grieve. It's good to review what we learn and write it down. Make a list of everything you learned about why death came into the world and who controls life and death. This will also give you a resource to come back to when you have questions in the future.

You may want to add to your list about God as well.

LESSON 8

Could I Have Prevented My Loved One's Death?

"Lord, if you had been here, my brother would not have died"
—Martha (John 11:21), Mary (32), and others (37)

In the first few months after our son died, we both had times of wondering if we had prayed more over our kids . . . or done more Bible Studies with them . . . or had more faith . . . or been better parents or better Christians . . . or not let Andrew go away to college at West Texas A & M University . . . or offered to drive him and his friends home from their End of Season cast   party . . . would he be alive today?

We don't know. What we do know is that none of our shortcomings caused The Accident. We have friends who might have prevented their children's accidental deaths. Our own adult son was killed because the "designated driver" of his car was intoxicated, unknown to our son. We would have done something differently had we known in advance the driver was incapable of safe driving, but we didn't. We cannot go back in time and change what happened. We accept this reality in the lives of others; we must accept it in our own lives as well. We know that God determines the number of our days. We also know we cannot change the past. What happened, happened, and we must learn how to live with it; if we don't it will drive us insane. If we made a critical mistake, we have to offer ourselves the same understanding we would extend to friends, hopefully so they would come to see that they did the best they could at the time.

What happened does not change who God is or what He has promised or what He has done and will do. As Job 1:21 says, "The Lord gave and the Lord has taken away. Blessed be the Lord."

For many, the loss of a loved one is accompanied with a sense of guilt, regret, and condemnation. You may be asking questions like we did—questions such as "Was it my fault he got sick?" "What would have happened if we had taken him to a different doctor?" "Did we feed him something that caused the illness?" "Should I have tried to stop her from using drugs?"

What do we do with these questions and doubts?

First, take time to honestly answer the questions that are plaguing you.

- Do you believe that feeding your child certain foods caused her to get cancer?

- Are you at fault for this?

- Could you have stopped the drunk driver from being on the road and hitting the car your family was in?

- Was it your fault your loved one got sick?

- Did you have any control over his choices of lifestyle, doctors, or medications?

- Could you have stopped her from using the substance she was addicted to?

Honestly assess the questions and doubts in your mind.

[Ron] For example, I struggled with guilt over our son's death in the vehicular accident. I wished I had gone to Canyon, Texas, and driven him and his friends to the End of the Season Party. Perhaps then the accident would have been prevented.

But it was unreasonable—a four-hour drive just to get to Canyon and the day-long Bar-B-Que at a ranch 90 minutes from there. Our son thought his "designated driver" was competent. I would have needed to take two days off work to drive over there, get Andrew, take him to the party, wait for him to be done at 11:00 pm, drive him back to his apartment for the night, and drive home the next day. It wasn't reasonable for me to do this.

Added to this, Andrew was a young man capable of making his own decisions. I came to see a glimpse of what I think our Heavenly Father feels: "Here are the keys, son; drive carefully," we say. Then we let them drive or choose who drives them, let them cook their own food and make other life-and-death decisions. Yes, it is terrifying, but that is what young adults must do. This showed me an aspect of God's love I had never considered: God's love is permissive: He lets his children do things that have consequences.

When you feel guilt, shame, and doubt, honestly assess their causes. Are you responsible for your loved one's death? How would you evaluate the responsibility of your friend who lost his loved one in identical circumstances? Would you assume he was doing the best he could in the critical situation?

You may feel that you or someone else contributed in some way to the death of your loved one. Beloved, God will help you determine whether these feelings are justified. He will show you the truth and give you wisdom if you have sinned or have something you need to make amends for. But understand that grief can lead us to assume we were somehow responsible even when this is totally unreasonable. Don't let grief fabricate facts. Don't blindly assume you "should have" done something to prevent their loss or that you need to do something now because of their loss. Instead, fully accept that you're really hurting and sad and then ask your loving Father to show you more.

Read James 1:5-6.

What does God promise?

Who does God give wisdom to? What condition(s) need to be met?

JAMES 1:5-6

5 If any of you lacks wisdom, let him ask God, who gives generously to all without reproach, and it will be given him. 6 But let him ask in faith, with no doubting, for the one who doubts is like a wave of the sea that is driven and tossed by the wind.

David cried out to God, "Search me, O God, and know my heart! Try me and know my thoughts! And see if there be any grievous way in me, and lead me in the way everlasting!" (Psalm 139:23-24). We can ask God to do this because He is loving and wants to transform us into the image of Christ.

All believers have the Holy Spirit in them (John 7:39; 1 Corinthians 12:13). Read John 16:7-8.

What does the Holy Spirit do for us?

JOHN 16:7-8

7 Nevertheless, I tell you the truth: it is to your advantage that I go away, for if I do not go away, the Helper will not come to you. But if I go, I will send him to you. 8 And when he comes, he will convict the world concerning sin and righteousness and judgment.

In 2 Corinthians 7 Paul mentions a previous letter he had sent (1 Corinthians). In that letter Paul rebuked the church for their wrong attitude toward their sin. Read 2 Corinthians 7:8-9.

Why did Paul come to rejoice?

2 CORINTHIANS 7:8-9

[8] *For even if I made you grieve with my letter, I do not regret it—though I did regret it, for I see that that letter grieved you, though only for a while.* [9] *As it is, I rejoice, not because you were grieved, but because you were grieved into repenting.*

Beloved, you may be feeling guilt, shame, or condemnation for something that happened. You may blame yourself for the death of your loved one. You must honestly assess the truth of this blame. If you did something wrong, if you sinned, the Holy Spirit will show you your sin. He will convict you concerning sin and righteousness. He does this so you can confess to God and receive His forgiveness rather than paralyze yourself with guilt. Paul says "there is now no condemnation for those who are in Christ Jesus" (Romans 8:1). We have to believe this truth, not our feelings. Truth sets us free (John 8:32).

The death of a loved one is not an easy thing. Many times we have all kinds of feelings and emotions about the events surrounding a death. We can trust God to help us deal with these emotions. Cry out to Him and ask Him for wisdom.

Before continuing on, take time to honestly assess the cause of your loved one's death. Did you play a role in it? In your Journal (see below), write what you are thinking and feeling about responsibility for your loved one's death.

Ask God to reveal truth to you. He will lovingly show you truth and reveal to you any wrongs you have done.

(If you are struggling with feelings of guilt or shame, you may need help from your pastor or a support group to come to terms with the truth of your situation. There is wisdom in seeking godly counsel.)

Just Journaling

Write in your Journal any feelings or guilt or shame you have regarding any responsibility for the death of your loved one. You may want to write a poem or draw a picture. Write a prayer asking God to show you the truth regarding any part you may have played in the death.

Thinking through Personal Responsibility

After honestly considering your responsibility in the death, there are three possible conclusions you can come to:

1. No, I did not cause the death; I had no responsibility at all.

2. Yes, I played a role in the death but it was not directly a result of my action or inaction.

3. Yes, I played a direct role in the death through my own choices and behavior.

We will look at these one at a time.

Option 1: You did not cause the death.

When we have doubts and sense guilt, if we are sure we did not sin or cause the death, we need to recognize where those accusations come from and we must not accept blame or condemnation.

First, remember that you are loved by God.

Next, read this passage and mark every mention of the *devil* with a pitchfork and references to God with a triangle. Note what you learn about the devil and how to deal with him.

The devil: nature, purposes, behavior

1 PETER 5:8-11

[8] Be sober-minded; be watchful. Your adversary the devil prowls around like a roaring lion, seeking someone to devour. [9] Resist him, firm in your faith, knowing that the same kinds of suffering are being experienced by your brotherhood throughout the world. [10] And after you have suffered a little while, the God of all grace, who has called you to his eternal glory in Christ, will himself restore, confirm,

The devil: nature, purposes, behavior

strengthen, and establish you. [11] To him be the dominion forever and ever. Amen.

2 CORINTHIANS 11:14

[14] And no wonder, for even Satan disguises himself as an angel of light.

JOHN 8:42-44

[42] Jesus said to them, "If God were your Father, you would love me, for I came from God and I am here. I came not of my own accord, but he sent me. [43] Why do you not understand what I say? It is because you cannot bear to hear my word. [44] You are of your father the devil, and your will is to do your father's desires. He was a murderer from the beginning, and does not stand in the truth, because there is no truth in him. When he lies, he speaks out of his own character, for he is a liar and the father of lies.

JAMES 4:7-8A

[7] Submit yourselves therefore to God. Resist the devil, and he will flee from you. [8] Draw near to God, and he will draw near to you.

Beloved, do not accept condemnation, guilt, or shame from the devil or from anyone else.

A few years ago we had something bad happen to one of our children. We were talking about the situation and Ron said, "I am not to blame for this and I will not accept blame from you or anyone else. You are not to blame for this. You should not accept blame. We will get through this together, you, me, and God." After Andrew died we remembered this exchange; it helps us to not blame each other for Andrew's death or accept blame from any other source.

If the enemy or another person tries to cause you to feel guilty, do not accept it. Know that you did not cause your loved one's death, and walk in the freedom of Christ. Submit to God during your grief, resist the devil when he speaks lies to you, and he will flee from you (James 4:7). Draw near to God in your suffering and He will draw near to you (v. 8).

Just Journaling

If you had no responsibility in the death which you are grieving, write that in your Journal. List anything you learned that you want to remember about Satan, anything that will help you heal in your grief.

Option 2: You played a role in the death but it was not directly a result of your action or inaction.

We have a friend who played a role in his daughter's death. It was a freak accident. He felt guilty because he thought that if he had been watching more carefully he might have been able to prevent it. For months he was wracked by guilt. It didn't help him to have others say "It was just an accident" or "God is in control." He needed relief from his guilt. Men often feel like they should have been stronger, they should have been the protector, they should have stopped their child's death. Our friend was feeling this way.

When we talked to him about considering any wrong he may have done, confessing it to God and to those impacted by the death, and then asking God and them for forgiveness, it was like a breath of fresh air for him. As it ended up, he realized he had *not* sinned, not done anything wrong; the death was simply a freak accident. He could have been watching more closely but we cannot always stop accidents from happening even *when* we are watching closely. He was sorry he had not been able to stop his child's death but he had not done anything wrong; he had done no sin to cause it.

He talked to God about it then told his wife and their other children how sorry he was about what happened. He talked to them about how they all missed their daughter and sister and how he wished it had not happened though it was no one's fault. He began to heal in his grief once he had taken these steps.

When thoughts of guilt creep back in, he recognizes them for what they are—lies from the enemy. He submits to God, resists the devil, and he flees from him. Sometimes this happens when he prays to God or praises Him, other times when he calls his wife or a friend who remind him of the truth and then pray with him. These tactics will work for you as well!

You may be thinking, "But I just can't forgive myself!" Beloved, nowhere in Scripture does God speak about "forgiving ourselves."

Read Psalm 51:4. David wrote this after his adulterous affair with Bathsheba.

How many persons does he say he sinned against?

PSALM 51:4

4 Against you, you only, have I sinned and done what is evil in your sight, so that you may be justified in your words and blameless in your judgment.

Now read Genesis 39:7-9.

Who does Joseph say he will be sinning against if he does what his master's wife wants?

GENESIS 39:7-9

7 And after a time his master's wife cast her eyes on Joseph and said, "Lie with me." 8 But he refused and said to his master's wife, "Behold, because of me my master has no concern about anything in the house, and he has put everything that he has in my charge. 9 He is not greater in this house than I am, nor has he kept back anything from me except you, because you are his wife. How then can I do this great wickedness and sin against God?"

Dear one, if you did sin, it was against God. Scripture is filled with examples of people confessing they sinned against God: Exodus 10:16, Joshua 7:20, and Judges 10:10 to name just a few. Ultimately, all sin is against God. It is His forgiveness we must seek, since the very definition of sin is rebellion against *His* Law (1 John 3:4). Scripture says "In him we have *redemption through his blood, the forgiveness of our trespasses,* according to the riches of his grace" (Ephesians 1:7, cf. Colossians 1:14). God did not simply say, "I forgive you." He sent His Son to pay the price for our sin, the sin of the whole world. *There is no forgiveness apart from this purchased redemption* and so John tells us to confess our sins to the only One who can cleanse us because He shed blood (1 John 1:7-9). Forgiveness includes sacrifice for sin and cleansing from it, things we can't do ourselves for ourselves.

When you say "I cannot forgive myself" you place yourself in the position of Judge, which is not for you. Judgment is *God's*. It may sound noble to say "God has forgiven me but I can't forgive myself," but when you do this you're putting yourself above God and there's nothing noble about that; it's pride. Similarly, if we have some responsibility in the death and don't admit it, we're sinning. We can't experience forgiveness and healing if we are not honest about our part.

So when God says "You are forgiven!" that is the end of the discussion! Stop beating yourself up. Stop placing yourself in the position of Judge. Trust Him. If you sinned, confess it to Him; believe His Son Jesus died for your sin, be cleansed by His blood and live in that forgiveness.

Just Journaling

Are you feeling guilt or shame regarding a death for which you hold no responsibility? Did you play a role in a death but not through sin? If so, write about your feelings. Then write the truth about what happened. Talk to God and ask Him to help you to remember the truth regarding the situation.

Option 3: Your action or inaction caused the death.

What can you do if your action or inaction, your sin, played a role in a death?

- If you turned your back on a child at the lake when you were in charge

- If you were driving intoxicated when family members were killed

- If you purposely killed someone in anger

- If you sinned in some other way which caused a death

The answer is the same anytime we sin: confess your sin, repent, ask forgiveness from God and those harmed by your actions, accept forgiveness, then go on living.

It is important to honestly admit the exact nature of our wrong. There should be no quibbling, no "but somebody else made me do it." On the other hand, we should not unquestioningly assign responsibility to ourselves. What *exactly* did we do and *why*? Honesty is essential.

After this assessment, if you decide you sinned confess it first to God. Ask His forgiveness. He will freely forgive anyone who truly repents. Then confess your sin to those you have hurt and ask their forgiveness.

The second part may seem impossible to do if the one you harmed is now dead. But you know without question the family of the victim was hurt. Then too, your own family and friends may have been harmed. Confess your sin to them and ask their forgiveness for the pain you caused them.

Then live.

Read the following passages. Mark the words *forgive, forgiveness, forgiven*, and *reconciled*. Underline *transgression, iniquity*, and *sin*.

Forgiveness

PSALM 32:1-7

[1] Blessed is the one whose transgression is forgiven, whose sin is covered. [2] Blessed is the man against whom the Lord counts no iniquity, and in whose spirit there is no deceit. [3] For when I kept silent, my bones wasted away through my groaning all day long. [4] For day and night your hand was heavy upon me; my strength was dried up as by the heat of summer. Selah [5] I acknowledged my sin to you, and I did not cover my iniquity; I said, "I will confess my transgressions to the Lord," and you forgave the iniquity of my sin. Selah [6] Therefore let everyone who is godly offer prayer to you at a time when you may be found; surely in the rush of great waters, they shall not reach him. [7] You are a hiding place for me; you preserve me from trouble; you surround me with shouts of deliverance. Selah

What does this passage say about the one whose transgression is forgiven?

According to verse 3 what happened to the Psalmist when he did not confess his sin, when he kept silent?

Who will forgive us?

What else will He do?

1 JOHN 1:8-9

8 If we say we have no sin, we deceive ourselves, and the truth is not in us. 9 If we confess our sins, he is faithful and just to forgive us our sins and to cleanse us from all unrighteousness.

From what you know about Scripture, on what basis are we forgiven and cleansed from all unrighteousness? Is it because of what we do?

What are we to do first when our brother has something against us?

MATTHEW 5:23-24

23 So if you are offering your gift at the altar and there remember that your brother has something against you, 24 leave your gift there before the altar and go. First be reconciled to your brother, and then come and offer your gift.

Read Romans 8:1, 31-39.

If you are a believer in Christ Jesus, are you condemned or forgiven?

List the things God does to forgive and save us. Note which are one-time and which are ongoing.

ROMANS 8:1, 31-39

1 There is therefore now no condemnation for those who are in Christ Jesus.

31 What then shall we say to these things? If God is for us, who can be against us? 32 He who did not spare his own Son but gave him up for us all, how will he not also with him graciously give us all things? 33 Who shall bring any charge against God's elect? It is God who justifies. 34 Who is to condemn? Christ Jesus is the one who died—more than that, who was raised—who is at the right hand of God, who indeed is interceding for us. 35 Who shall separate us from the love of Christ? Shall tribulation, or distress, or persecution, or famine, or nakedness, or danger, or sword? 36 As it is written,

List the things that cannot separate us from the love of God in Christ Jesus our Lord.

How do you feel about these promises?

"For your sake we are being killed all the day long; we are regarded as sheep to be slaughtered." [37] No, in all these things we are more than conquerors through him who loved us. [38] For I am sure that neither death nor life, nor angels nor rulers, nor things present nor things to come, nor powers, [39] nor height nor depth, nor anything else in all creation, will be able to separate us from the love of God in Christ Jesus our Lord.

If you sinned and caused a death, forgiveness is available.

If your actions were illegal you may face legal penalties such as fines or jail time. You may face civil action such as a lawsuit. These do not mean you will face eternal condemnation for your actions. Jesus said, "For God so loved the world, that he gave his only Son, that whoever believes in him should not perish but have eternal life. For God did not send his Son into the world to condemn the world, but in order that the world might be saved through him" (John 3:16-17).

Friend, if you are in some way responsible for a death, honestly assess whether you sinned or if it was just a bad situation. If you did not sin, do not allow the enemy to lie to you and condemn you. If you sinned there is forgiveness through Christ. Confess your sin. Ask God for forgiveness and then walk in the freedom that comes from being a child of God, *even if you're in prison!*

If you played a role in a death, whatever your level of responsibility was you can be free from condemnation. You can choose to "go, and sin no more" (John 8:11). You can choose to live a life of faith in Jesus Christ.

GALATIANS 5:1

For freedom Christ has set us free; stand firm therefore, and do not submit again to a yoke of slavery.

Read Isaiah 45:5-7.

What is God sovereign over?

ISAIAH 45:5-7

[5] *I am the L*ORD*, and there is no other, besides me there is no God; I equip you, though you do not know me,* [6] *that people may know, from the rising of the sun and from the west, that there is none besides me; I am the* LORD*, and there is no other.* [7] *I form light and create darkness, I make well-being and create calamity, I am the* LORD*, who does all these things.*

This is a difficult truth for all of us. It's hard to reconcile a God who loves us with the fact that He controls life and death. Dear one, God's hand is in everything; He causes well-being and calamity. You may have sinned and played a role in the death of someone you deeply care for but ultimately God is the One who controls life and death. If you sinned, confess and repent. Accept God's forgiveness. Then continue to "work out your salvation with fear and trembling," knowing He loves you enough to give His Son for you and with Him . . . "all things" (Romans 8:32).

Just Journaling

If you sinned and caused a death, write in your Journal the truth about forgiveness. You may want to look up additional verses regarding what Jesus did for you and the forgiveness that is available to you. If you need to confess anything to God, do so. Ask forgiveness. Write in your Journal that today you have been forgiven.

One final point. Sometimes when a loved one dies we feel guilt over things we said or did to them. We wish we could go back and unsay things or do things differently. This is especially true for us who have dealt with family members or friends in addiction. We wish we could have stopped them. We wish we could have had a better relationship with them. We can't. They're gone now. This is hard to deal with, but it is what it is.

My friend, if you treated someone poorly or the last words you spoke to someone were in anger, go back and read the last few pages of this lesson.

Confess your sin to God, ask forgiveness, and live in the freedom of Christ! You cannot change the past but you can determine how you will live today. With the help of the Holy Spirit you can set your mind on things above. You can be led by the Spirit and walk in the Spirit. You can be kind and compassionate to others, forgiving them just as in Christ God forgave you.

Just Journaling

If the last words you spoke to loved ones who died were in anger or if you feel shame over the way you treated them and you can't shake the guilt, consider writing it down as a confession, an apology, to the person and to God.

Pour out your heart, everything that is troubling your conscience. Then read it aloud to God. Tell Him you are sorry. Ask His forgiveness. Tell Him you are coming to him by the book of Jesus as Hebrews 10:19-22 says. Thank HIm that you have a great priest over the house of God—Jesus—and you want to draw near to Him with a sincere heart in full assurance of faith, having your heart sprinkled clean from an evil conscience and your body washed with pure water.

Then if you can get on your knees, thank your Father and His Son for so great a salvation and write 1 John 1:9 over what you've written. Tuck the letter away and if the thought comes back, get it out and read it again aloud —and tell the Accuser of the brethren, the devil, to be gone.

LESSON 9

Welcoming God's Transformation in Grief

Do not be conformed to this world, but be transformed by the renewal of your mind, that by testing you may discern what is the will of God, what is good and acceptable and perfect (Romans 12:2).

Perhaps at this point the following principles have begun to settle in your heart:

- God is good, loving, full of compassion and mercy

- We can trust Him to heal us in our grief

- The Fall of Man brought sin, death, and trouble into the world

- God controls life and death

- The Word of God contains answers to our questions about life and death

- I can learn to live with peace and joy by seeking God, studying the Bible, and applying truth in my life

If you believe these things, are you open to God's working and transformation in your life during this situation?

God works through our suffering to perfect us, to make us mature. From Scripture we learn that it's the normal process for the Christian. While this may not be widely embraced in the Church, it's abundantly clear in the Word.

According to the Bible suffering is part of the Christian life; God uses it to do significant work in our lives. Read these passages and underline references to *suffering* and *testing*. List what you learn about suffering and testing.

Suffering and Testing	**1 PETER 5:10**
	¹⁰ And after you have suffered a little while, the God of all grace, who has called you to his eternal glory in

Suffering and Testing

Christ, will himself restore, confirm, strengthen, and establish you.

JAMES 1:3-4

³ for you know that the testing of your faith produces steadfastness. ⁴ And let steadfastness have its full effect, that you may be perfect and complete, lacking in nothing.

ROMANS 5:3-5

³ Not only that, but we rejoice in our sufferings, knowing that suffering produces endurance, ⁴ and endurance produces character, and character produces hope, ⁵ and hope does not put us to shame, because God's love has been poured into our hearts through the Holy Spirit who has been given to us.

2 CORINTHIANS 4:11

¹¹ For we who live are always being given over to death for Jesus' sake, so that the life of Jesus also may be manifested in our mortal flesh.

Through suffering Christ restores, confirms, strengthens, and establishes us (1 Peter 5:10). The testing of our faith produces steadfastness (endurance) through which we're perfected (completed), lacking nothing (James 1:3-4). Suffering produces endurance, character, and hope (Romans 5:3-5). All of this is so that the life of Jesus will be revealed in our mortal flesh (2 Corinthians 4:11).

Read the following passages. Underline *suffering, suffer,* and circle *transformed* and *transformation.*

List what you learn about suffering and transformation.

What did you learn about Jesus in this passage?

How did Jesus learn obedience?

If Jesus learned obedience through suffering, how do you think you will?

Is spiritual sight important?

Who do disciples become like?

How will you be transformed?

What is the result of transformation?

HEBREWS 5:7-9

⁷ In the days of his flesh, Jesus offered up prayers and supplications, with loud cries and tears, to him who was able to save him from death, and he was heard because of his reverence. ⁸ Although he was a son, he learned obedience through what he suffered. ⁹ And being made perfect, he became the source of eternal salvation to all who obey him,

LUKE 6:40

³⁹ He also told them a parable: "Can a blind man lead a blind man? Will they not both fall into a pit? ⁴⁰ A disciple is not above his teacher, but everyone when he is fully trained will be like his teacher.

ROMANS 12:2

² Do not be conformed to this world, but be transformed by the renewal of your mind, that by testing you may discern what is the will of God, what is good and acceptable and perfect.

The unveiled face is one who has recognized the only way to salvation is Christ Jesus.

What happens to us as we behold Christ's glory?

2 CORINTHIANS 3:18

18 And we all, with unveiled face, beholding the glory of the Lord, are being transformed into the same image from one degree of glory to another. For this comes from the Lord who is the Spirit.

Is Paul telling the Corinthians to be like him?

1 CORINTHIANS 11:1

1 Be imitators of me, as I am of Christ.

Who are we to imitate *ultimately?*

Now, looking back at the previous verses, how do we learn to imitate Christ?

In the following Paul is writing to "the churches of Galatia" (Galatians 1:2). Some in these churches have turned away from the true gospel. Paul writes to correct them and remind them to hold to the true gospel of Jesus Christ.

According to this verse, what is Paul's ultimate desire for them?

GALATIANS 4:19

19 my little children, for whom I am again in the anguish of childbirth until Christ is formed in you!

How "desirous" is he?

Does he anticipate some quick and easy process?

How does he describe it?

What do potters do with clay?

JEREMIAH 18:1-4

[1] *The word that came to Jeremiah from the LORD:* [2] *"Arise, and go down to the potter's house, and there I will let you hear my words."* [3] *So I went down to the potter's house, and there he was working at his wheel.* [4] *And the vessel he was making of clay was spoiled in the potter's hand, and he reworked it into another vessel, as it seemed good to the potter to do.*

What did this potter do with the spoiled vessel?

How are we saved?

EPHESIANS 2:8-10

[8] *For by grace you have been saved through faith. And this is not your own doing; it is the gift of God,* [9] *not a result of works, so that no one may boast.* [10] *For we are his workmanship, created in Christ Jesus for good works, which God prepared beforehand, that we should walk in them.*

According to verse 10, why were we created?

What do you learn about these "works"?

God goes on to warn the nation of Israel that He can do as He pleases with His creation. He says, "If at any time I declare concerning a nation or a kingdom, that I will pluck up and break down and destroy it, and if that nation, concerning which I have spoken, turns from its evil, I will relent of the disaster that I intended to do to it" (Jeremiah 18:7-8).

God makes it clear that He's the potter and we're the clay; He decides what to make of us. He tells us in 2 Corinthians 3:18 and Galatians 4:19 that He is transforming us into the image of Christ. This transforming work may be uncomfortable at times but we can trust Him to perfect this perfect image in us.

Read the following verses and mark *God* including synonyms and pronouns that refer to Him with a triangle. Note what you learn.

God

PSALM 103:13-14

¹³ *As a father shows compassion to his children, so the* LORD *shows compassion to those who fear Him.* ¹⁴ *For he knows our frame; he remembers that we are dust.*

1 CORINTHIANS 8:5-6

⁵ *For although there may be so-called gods in heaven or on earth—as indeed there are many "gods" and many "lords"—* ⁶ *yet for us there is one God, the Father, from whom are all things and for whom we exist, and one Lord, Jesus Christ, through whom are all things and through whom we exist.*

PSALM 68:5

⁵ *Father of the fatherless and protector of widows is God in his holy habitation.*

1 PETER 1:3-4

³ *Blessed be the God and Father of our Lord Jesus Christ! According to his great mercy, he has caused us to be born again to a living hope through the resurrection of Jesus Christ from the dead,* ⁴ *to an inheritance that is imperishable, undefiled, and unfading, kept in heaven for you,*

God is a good Father who loves you and is full of mercy and compassion for you. You can trust Him to transform you into the image of His Son.

Trusting God is an act of faith that takes effort. It requires us to seek Him, learn about Him from studying His Word, and then applying what we learn in our daily lives. Each day we must choose to do the next right thing, the thing God has put in front of us. "For we are God's handiwork, created in Christ Jesus to do good works, which God prepared in advance for us to do" (Ephesians 2:10).

You were asked early in this study to start a list of things you learned about God. Knowing God's nature will give you true and lasting peace. Your list of who God is and what He has done is a permanent resource for dark times, times of doubting and confusion. When you are hurting you can reach for your *Journal* and review your list. It will be like soothing medicine for your soul, dear one.

If you haven't started this list, turn to the back of your *Journal* and on the designated page begin to list everything you have learned about God. When you have time go back through lessons 1-8 and write down what you learned about God and what he has done. Include the promises of what He will do as well, then cling to those promises. He is a promise-making, promise-keeping God! Be sure to write verse references next to your insights so you can find them in the Bible later. It will take some time and effort to do this, but it's well worth it!

Just Journaling

If you have not kept up with your list of "What I Learned About God," now's a good time to update it. Then, continue with this lesson.

Transformation is a Lifetime Process but It Begins Today If You Are Willing

Has someone ever said to you, "Take all the time you need; there's no time limit to grief" or "You don't need to work on spiritual things right now, just concentrate on dealing with your grief"?

Beloved, there is no time limit on grief. God is not in a hurry; He wants to do a transforming work in you that will take your lifetime. But if during our suffering we don't seek God by studying His Word and applying it, if we don't pray and worship we will not find healing in our grief. To neglect such things is to say "I don't want to make my ear attentive to God's wisdom. I don't want to call out to God for insight, not right now while I'm hurting." But this is exactly when we need God's wisdom and insight—*while* we go through the trials! We need to apply truth in our lives in order to persevere and receive the crown of life God promised to those who love Him. We must apply His truth in our lives during suffering to find God's healing in our grief. Go back to the fundamental principles we stated at the beginning of this lesson and reconsider your perspective.

Does this seem harsh or inappropriate for someone grieving, someone recovering from a very painful situation—to tell them they need to turn their heart towards God and welcome His work in their life not only as Comforter but also as Lord? Is it harsh to say He is God and does as He pleases?

My friend, if we want God to gently guide us to healing in our grief, we must remember the mercy and compassion of Jesus. If God is "kind to the ungrateful and wicked" (Luke 6:35), don't you think He'll heal and restore those who are his sons (Galatians 3:26)? Grief is a huge part of your life right now. Do you think this situation is incompatible with God working in your life? As we willingly seek the Comforter, is it not inevitable that we will find ourselves conformed to the image of the Lord Jesus who suffered? Didn't Paul say "For it has been granted to you that for the sake of Christ you should not only believe in him but also suffer for his sake" (Philippians 1:29)? As uncomfortable as this transformation may be, *it is worth it!*

We must be honest, open-minded, and willing to understand the freedom Paul speaks about in 2 Corinthians 3:17. The Holy Spirit is the Master Builder (like Paul in 1 Corinthians 3:10). He builds His people (the Church) on the ultimate foundation, the Lord Jesus Christ. He will transform us for God's glory and our ultimate benefit through good times and bad. That is why we are told to "count it all joy" *in* our situation, not to be glad *of the situation itself* (James 1:4).

Many of us have found the sweetest experiences with God in the middle of our suffering, much like the "treasure in jars of clay" Paul described:

2 CORINTHIANS 4:7-10

⁷ But we have this treasure in jars of clay, to show that the surpassing power belongs to God and not to us. ⁸ We are afflicted in every way, but not crushed; perplexed, but not driven to despair; ⁹ persecuted, but not forsaken; struck down, but not destroyed; ¹⁰ always carrying in the body the death of Jesus, so that the life of Jesus may also be manifested in our bodies.

If we want to change our way of walking, we first have to change our way of thinking, which is what "repentance" means. God's kindness leads us to repentance (Romans 2:4). "Repent for the Kingdom of Heaven is at hand" is not a threat, but a glorious announcement: "Change your way of thinking, a whole new way of life is now available to you!"

ROMANS 2:4

⁴ Or do you presume on the riches of his kindness and forbearance and patience, not knowing that God's kindness is meant to lead you to repentance?

[Ron] When we are pressured the inside of us squeezes out. This is inevitable though I personally find it very disturbing. But our Father is not surprised. He sees these things and so much more, long before we even conceive them. He offers us forgiveness and a new life. Will you work out what He works in you (Philippians 2:12-13) as He transforms you into the image of His Son? If so, let's get to work right now changing our thoughts, the topic of our next lesson.

Just Journaling

<u>First</u>, *looking back over what you learned in the first part of this study, what has impacted you the most? What surprised or comforted you the most?*

<u>Second</u>, *what changes have you seen in your grief over the weeks you have been studying God's Word? Are you seeing God's healing in your grief? Describe what you are seeing. Maybe draw a picture, write a poem, or compose a song.*

<u>Finally</u>, *if you are willing to work out what God is working in as He transforms you, write about it in your Journal. You may want to write a prayer asking God to continue to work in and through you.*

LESSON 10

Changing Our Thoughts

You keep him in perfect peace whose mind is stayed on you, because he trusts in you (Isaiah 26:3).

Many of us who have lost loved ones have trouble stopping the dark thoughts, the flashbacks, and the "What if?"s. Sometimes we think about what we would have done differently and the regrets we have over things we actually did. Sometimes we blame ourselves or others for what happened. We may be very angry about what happened or over the very fact that our loved ones died. We replay conversations we had with them and with people who were trying to comfort and help us. We replay conversations we *wish* we'd had with our loved ones before they died. These dark thoughts sometimes cause us to lash out at others.

Trying to get to sleep at night when all we can think about is death and the pain of missing our loved ones is really tough! Even during the day, we often have trouble thinking about anything other than our personal loss and suffering. Because this is what we think about, it's also what we talk about. We can talk about it so much that it alienates others who are hurting and in need of comfort.

Some of us were at the accident site and saw the broken bodies. Others cared for their loved ones as they drew closer to death. Others were in the Emergency Room or ICU watching medical staff try to resuscitate their parent or child. The images we have in our minds play over and over like a very bad movie.

It's hard to stop thinking about death, grief, and our pain after losing a loved one. We may fear that someone else we love will die. We may come to fear death generally.

These memories and thoughts can lead to anxiety, anger, and depression. What we really need is peace and comfort from God.

What do we do when our thoughts turn to dark difficult places?

We need to set our minds on better things, different things. We need to trust God and set our minds on things above, things of the Spirit that are defined in the Word of God. On these things God's Word tells us to "set your mind" (Colossians 3:2), "set your mind and heart" (1 Chronicles 22:19), "think about" (Philippians 4:8) and, generally, "be transformed by the renewal of your mind" (Romans 12:2). "Yes Lord, I want to do this, I need to, please help me" is a great prayer.

As we saw in the last lesson, while faith is a gift from God (Romans 12:3; Philippians 1:29) it's an effort we make. It requires us to learn the objects of faith (God's nature and God's works) from studying His Word and applying it in our lives.

Read the following passages, underline every *we* or *us*. Draw a heart over the word *love* and note what you learn about God's love for you.

What has God done for us?

ROMANS 8:31-35

31 What then shall we say to these things? If God is for us, who can be against us? 32 He who did not spare his own Son but gave him up for us all, how will he not also with him graciously give us all things? 33 Who shall bring any charge against God's elect? It is God who justifies. 34 Who is to condemn? Christ Jesus is the one who died—more than that, who was raised—who is at the right hand of God, who indeed is interceding for us. 35 Who shall separate us from the love of Christ? Shall tribulation, or distress, or persecution, or famine, or nakedness, or danger, or sword?

What is His fundamental attitude towards us?

What has Jesus done for us?

What's the big consequence of these actions by the Father and the Son?

1 JOHN 3:1

[1] See what kind of love the Father has given to us, that we should be called children of God; and so we are.

EPHESIANS 1:3-6

[3] Blessed be the God and Father of our Lord Jesus Christ, who has blessed us in Christ with every spiritual blessing in the heavenly places, [4] even as he chose us in him before the foundation of the world, that we should be holy and blameless before him. In love [5] he predestined us for adoption to himself as sons through Jesus Christ, according to the purpose of his will, [6] to the praise of his glorious grace, with which he has blessed us in the Beloved.

God loves you. All who believe in Jesus are God's children. You were chosen before the foundation of the world to be adopted as His son! He is a good Father. When you're suffering, remember these things: God loves you and wants what is best for you, as any loving father does for his own children.

Knowing we are loved by God, redeemed by Christ, and adopted as sons and joint heirs brings great comfort.

Set Your Minds on Things Above

So how do we change our thoughts? How do we stop thinking dark thoughts? How do we stop thinking about death, pain, sorrow, and ugly things? Friend, it's not within our will-power to do this; we can't *will* dark thoughts away. We can't *will* thoughts of sorrow, pain, regret, or anger to stop. We can't simply stop thinking about our loved one's death. Suppression (commanding ourselves "Don't think about that!") typically reinforces negativism. Likewise, a direct frontal attack on self-destructive thinking (and other bad habits) rarely succeeds. Instead, we must train ourselves to think differently, think other things. What things? What should we practice thinking about? The Word of God gives us specific instructions that are helpful.

Read these passages. Circle the words *minds* and *mind*. Note what you learn about the mind.

What is the result of setting the mind on the Spirit?

ROMANS 8:5-6

5 For those who live according to the flesh set their minds on the things of the flesh, but those who live according to the Spirit set their minds on the things of the Spirit. 6 For to set the mind on the flesh is death, but to set the mind on the Spirit is life and peace.

What are we to seek, set our minds on?

COLOSSIANS 3:1-4

1 If then you have been raised with Christ, seek the things that are above, where Christ is, seated at the right hand of God. 2 Set your minds on things that are above, not on things that are on earth. 3 For you have died, and your life is hidden with Christ in God. 4 When Christ who is your life appears, then you also will appear with him in glory.

Why?

How are we transformed or changed?

ROMANS 12:1-2

1 I appeal to you therefore, brothers, by the mercies of God, to present your bodies as a living sacrifice, holy and acceptable to God, which is your spiritual worship. 2 Do not be conformed to this world, but be transformed by the renewal of your mind, that by testing you may discern what is the will of God, what is good and acceptable and perfect.

What does God do when we set our minds on Him?

ISAIAH 26:3-4

3 You keep him in perfect peace whose mind is stayed on you, because he trusts in you. 4 Trust in the Lord forever, for the Lord God is an everlasting rock.

All these passages tell us to set our minds on things above for our benefit. We should obey instructions that are for our own good. We will find peace when believe the Word of God and apply it in our lives.

What does "set your mind on things above" mean? Let's look at Colossians 3. This passage clearly tells us what the "earthly things in you [us]" are. We also learn what we are to put on as God's chosen ones.

Read the passage and underline *put to death, put away, do not, put on, let* and *do*. Mark other key words then answer the questions.

What are we to:

put to death?

put away?

not do?

put on?

COLOSSIANS 3:5-17

5 Put to death therefore what is earthly in you: sexual immorality, impurity, passion, evil desire, and covetousness, which is idolatry. 6 On account of these the wrath of God is coming. 7 In these you too once walked, when you were living in them. 8 But now you must put them all away: anger, wrath, malice, slander, and obscene talk from your mouth. 9 Do not lie to one another, seeing that you have put off the old self with its practices 10 and have put on the new self, which is being renewed in knowledge after the image of its creator. 11 Here there is not Greek and Jew, circumcised and uncircumcised, barbarian, Scythian, slave, free; but Christ is all, and in all. 12 Put on then, as God's chosen ones, holy and beloved, compassionate hearts, kindness, humility, meekness, and patience, 13 bearing with one another

What are we to:

put on?

and, if one has a complaint against another, forgiving each other; as the Lord has forgiven you, so you also must forgive. *14* And above all these put on love, which binds everything together in perfect harmony. *15* And let the peace of Christ rule in your hearts, to which indeed you were called in one body. And be thankful. *16* Let the word of Christ dwell in you richly, teaching and admonishing one another in all wisdom, singing psalms and hymns and spiritual songs, with thankfulness in your hearts to God. *17* And whatever you do, in word or deed, do everything in the name of the Lord Jesus, giving thanks to God the Father through him.

let?

do?

My friend, should we think "earthly" thoughts, do "earthly" actions? If you're regularly thinking about these, have you put them to death or are you keeping them alive in your mind?

What does the Word of Christ do in us?

Looking back over these passages, do you see any qualifications or exceptions in these instructions? For example, do we get "a pass" to *not* do these "put off" "put on" things when we're hurting, grieving, suffering?

Beloved, can you put on a compassionate heart towards those around you even when you're grieving? Can you rid yourself of anger, wrath, malice, slander, and obscene talk? This may seem impossible! But with the help of the Holy Spirit, we can do what the Bible tells us to do, even as we grieve. Paul wrote in Philippians 4:12-13, "I know how to be brought low, and I know how to abound. In any and every circumstance, I have learned the secret of facing plenty and hunger, abundance and need. I can do all things through him who strengthens me." This can be your experience as well.

Trials and loss have made Ron and I more compassionate toward others. Before these trials we tended to negatively judge others going through difficult times. But now we're compassionate toward them since we've experienced similar if not equal losses and sufferings. We've learned obedience through suffering, putting on kindness, humility, meekness, and patience in spite of our troubles. We bear with one another and with those around us better, with more patience and gentleness. We are more forgiving. We learned to give thanks to God the Father through Christ during our hard times and grief. These are results from setting our minds on things above, the things of the Spirit.

Are you willing to do what it takes to be transformed in your thinking? If so, pray; ask God to transform, renew, remake you.

Just Journaling

Summarize what you learned from Colossians 3. List what you are to "put on" and what you are "put off [and 'away']." Ask God to help you apply what you have learned.

Do Not Fear

In a previous lesson we looked at why people die. We learned that God numbers our days, but you may still fear losing another family member. What can you do when thoughts of future loss and other fears dominate your mind?

Setting our minds on God's Word helps us conquer our fears. Knowing and trusting truth from His Word replaces anxiety and fear of the future with peace. Beloved, studying and applying truths from Scripture will help you overcome *your* fears. Go back and review what you learned about God's sovereignty over life and death in lessons 6 and 7. Then review all you know about Him. When you're done, ask yourself this: "Can I trust Him with my life? Can I trust Him with those I love?" God's Word says He's trustworthy; that's what He says about Himself. He's a good, loving, kind Father. God alone is faithful and worthy of our trust!

Fear is in our minds; it's specific thought (dread about some bad future) but it's always speculative. When we fear losing another loved one, we *assume what will happen* rather than *think what is true now*. There are hundreds of verses about fear in the Bible. We're going to look at a few of them.

As you read through these verses, mark the word *fear* and the phrase *fear not* in a distinct way and note what you learn about it. Be sure to add to your list of things you learn about God.

Fear

PSALM 27:1

¹ The Lᴏʀᴅ is my light and my salvation; whom shall I fear? The Lᴏʀᴅ is the stronghold of my life; of whom shall I be afraid?

PSALM 56:3-4

³ When I am afraid, I put my trust in you. ⁴ In God, whose word I praise, in God I trust; I shall not be afraid. What can flesh do to me?

2 TIMOTHY 1:6-7

⁶ For this reason I remind you to fan into flame the gift of God, which is in you through the laying on of my hands ⁷ for God gave us a spirit not of fear but of power and love and self-control.

1 JOHN 4:18a

¹⁸ There is no fear in love, but perfect love casts out fear.

According to Romans 8, who/what are sons of God?

ROMANS 8:14-17

¹⁴ For all who are led by the Spirit of God are sons of God. ¹⁵ For you did not receive the spirit of slavery to fall back into fear, but you have received the Spirit of adoption as sons, by whom we cry, "Abba! Father!" ¹⁶ The Spirit himself bears witness with our spirit that we are children of God, ¹⁷ and if children, then heirs—heirs of God and fellow heirs with Christ, provided we suffer with him in order that we may also be glorified with him.

What does this mean for you if you're a believer?

According to verse 17, what are those who suffer with Christ promised?

Beloved, fear not! Yes, we will suffer in this life on earth, but if we keep our minds set on the things of the Spirit, if we're led by that Spirit, we are sons of God, destined to peace and fellow heirs with Christ. If we suffer with Christ, we're destined to glory with Him!

> *[Kathleen] One way to relieve suffering is to turn our thoughts into prayers. When I think about how much I miss my dad or my son, I pray. I tell God I miss them and thank Him for giving them to me, for letting me be my dad's daughter and my son's mom. When I'm afraid I turn to the Lord in prayer, asking Him to give me wisdom and peace. Sometimes I write what I'm thinking in a Journal and turn that into a prayer.*

Take time to write a prayer to God, expressing your concerns and fears. Maybe you'd prefer to write a poem or draw a picture that represents your fears and how God can help you conquer them.

Just Journaling

Are you afraid of losing another family member or friend? Look up "fear" and "fear not" in your Bible's concordance or in an online one. Then look up verses about fear and trusting God. Copy some of both into your Journal. Then turn them into a prayer or poem, asking God to help you trust Him and not fear.

What Should We Think About?

Read Philippians 4:4-9. According to verses 4-5 what should we do and why?

How far away is the Lord according to verse 5?

What does verse 6 say about being anxious? What does it tell us to do instead?

What will happen according to verse 7?

PHILIPPIANS 4:4-9

[4] *Rejoice in the Lord always; again I will say, rejoice.* [5] *Let your reasonableness be known to everyone. The Lord is at hand;* [6] *do not be anxious about anything, but in everything by prayer and supplication with thanksgiving let your requests be made known to God.* [7] *And the peace of God, which surpasses all understanding, will guard your hearts and your minds in Christ Jesus.* [8] *Finally, brothers, whatever is true, whatever is honorable, whatever is just, whatever is pure, whatever is lovely, whatever is commendable,*

Also according to 7, what will happen | *if there is any excellence, if there is*
to your mind (thought) if you do what | *anything worthy of praise, think about*
verses 4-6 tell us to do? | *these things. ⁹ What you have learned*
| *and received and heard and seen in*
| *me—practice these things, and the God*
| *of peace will be with you.*

Verse 8 tells you to think about certain things. List them.

Verse 9 tells us to do one more thing. What is it and what will happen?

Note that this passage does not tell us to rejoice that our loved one is gone, to be happy with this circumstance. Nor does it tell us to be glad that we're hurting and grieving. Look again, carefully, at verse 4. Who or what are we to rejoice in?

We can't simply stop thinking about our loss and pain. They are stuck in the forefront of our minds because of inevitable associations. For example, in the weeks and months after a death there are many tasks to be done that keep our loss front and center in our minds—legal issues, helping family members who are hurting, paying expenses from our loved one's death and funeral, dealing with their belongings, and much more. We have to think about these things to get them all done.

But we also need peace. We need the comfort God offers. We need to heal as we grieve. In order to begin to heal and find peace again, we need to replace our thoughts of *what we lost* with thoughts of *what we had, what we still have,* and *what we will have* in Christ. This is not done easily, especially immediately after a loss. We need time to process our loss and feel the pain. But over time as we turn to God for comfort, our very thought-life will change.

Do you need the peace of God? Do you want it? If you're anxious today, if you're feeling no peace, take time to pray. Take your pain, grief, anxiety all to Our Heavenly Father. Consider writing out your prayer here or in your *Journal*.

We can't just turn off the images in our minds. We can't simply stop being afraid. We must instead replace these by setting our minds on other thoughts and images, God's thoughts and images. We must choose to think about these superior things.

> *[Ron] You may find it helpful to write out and memorize a few things and use them to develop new thought patterns that can become habitual. For example, when I start to replay the gruesome thoughts of my son's death (a grossly misdirected meditation), I choose to recount mental images of him dancing, laughing, and playing. This is easier when I review photos or videos of him doing those things but I also have strong images in memory that I simply need to recall and focus upon. For example, in at least two dance performances, Andrew danced around the stage with knives or axes (don't ask me to explain, it was Dramatic Dance). He was known to be a little clumsy off-stage. I laugh out loud when I remember that fact and replay in my mind the movies of him gracefully moving around the stage with knives and axes.*
>
> *If I start telling myself an untrue narrative about his life or death, I practice repeating a contrary narrative supported by Scripture I know to be true and valuable. It's easier when I write it out and memorize it. This memorized seed of thought grows into more positive recollections. The product of healthier meditation aligned with God's Word is new, healing thought patterns. This is not "New-Age positive thinking." Setting my mind on (aligning my thoughts with) truth is the healthy practice of God developing "the mind of Christ" in me.*

It's not easy to do but with time, as we align our thoughts with truth, the domineering thoughts of our loss lessen and thoughts of good things in our life, joy and peace, increase and take over. This does not mean we forget our loss, our loved ones. But as we grow and heal, the very same thoughts of them that earlier oppressed and sorrowed us begin to bring us peace and joy. It may seem hard for you to believe now, but this is how God healed us.

We learned years ago to make a list of good things to think about based on Philippians 4:8. This helps us stop thinking Dark thoughts and start thinking Light ones. We choose to think the items on our list.

Here is Kathleen's list today:

True: It's true that Andrew loved me. I loved him. It's true that he has always been loved by the Lord and still is and that he's loved by believers from all ages he has joined including many still here on earth, Christians and non-Christians we hope will someday turn to Christ. It's true that he's alive in the presence of Christ. It's true that our parents loved us and we are grateful for this legacy in our lives.

Honorable: It's honorable for me to bite my tongue and not say everything I feel or think. It's honorable when others help me through the hard days with kindness. It was honorable when I was patient with a difficult person yesterday.

Right: It's right for me to be kind to others even when I'm in pain. It's right for me to ignore provocative words I can easily get angry about. It's right for me to get dressed today and good for me to brush my teeth, since I have to go out in public.

Pure: The love I receive from God is pure. The giggles of my granddaughter are pure delight!

Lovely: The blue sky and the green trees in springtime are lovely creatures! A hummingbird eating from one of our red flowers is lovely. The knowing, sweet smile of a new bereaved friend is lovely. Seeing an elderly couple holding hands and grinning at each other is lovely. The kindness a caregiver gave to a hurting older gentleman in the doctor's office this morning was lovely.

Commendable: The way many of you handle your loss and still show grace and kindness is commendable. The way my oldest daughter parents her children despite her having a very imperfect mom is commendable.

Excellent: The grace of God is excellent. God's Word is excellent. The way my husband loves me though he too is hurting is excellent. My son's smile was excellent, as were his dancing and his laugh.

Praiseworthy: A kind word, a job well done, and a gentle answer to an insult are all praiseworthy. Friends who keep calling and texting to check on me is praiseworthy.

Friends, can you make a list of things that are true, honorable, right, pure, lovely, commendable, excellent, and praiseworthy in your life?

Below is the list of godly attributes from Philippians 4:8. Under each write something you can choose to think about when dark thoughts creep into your mind. Make a list of good things in your life. Make a list of things other than your pain and grief that you can think about when you begin to feel anxious, angry, fearful, or upset. You may even want to copy some to 3 x 5 index cards and keep them with you to review daily.

True

Honorable

Just

Pure

Lovely

Commendable

Excellent

Praiseworthy

Just Journaling

In your Journal you will find these attributes listed. You may want to copy the list you just made there. As you go through the rest of this study, take time to think about those things that are true, honorable, just, pure, lovely, commendable, excellent, and praiseworthy in your life. Add to your list on the designated pages of your Journal. You will be amazed at all the wonderful things in your life, all the wonderful things you can think about and praise God for giving you!

LESSON 11

Gratitude in Grief

You will be sorrowful, but your sorrow will turn into joy (John 16:20b).

In the last lesson we looked at how to change our thoughts by keeping our mind set on the things of the Spirit rather than on earthly things. We practiced choosing to think about things that are true, noble, right, pure, lovely, commendable, excellent and praiseworthy.

Another way to change our thoughts is to choose gratitude for what we have instead of thinking only about our loss.

In the early days and weeks of grief our loss is primary in our minds; we are hurting. It is natural to think and talk about our loss; that's part of the healing process. We need to feel the sorrow and process what has happened. We need to discuss our loss with others who will understand—our spouses, pastors, and friends. Sometimes a Christian grief counselor can help us as we process our emotions and thoughts.

At some point, however, we must begin to change our thoughts from what we have *lost* to gratitude for what we *have* in order to heal. We must choose to think about life and living rather than death and dying. We have family and friends who need us and love us. It is important that we choose life despite our pain and that we continue to do the good works God has for us to do. Our family and friends need us in their lives and want us to be available to them with joy and peace.

We must also remember that "death is swallowed up in victory" (1 Corinthians 15:54), that when a grain of wheat falls in the ground and dies it brings forth much fruit (John 12:24). We must think the right thoughts about death. It's "the last enemy," granted, but it will be destroyed (1 Corinthians 15:26).

[Kathleen] For the first ten months after The Accident I got very depressed around the twelfth. The Accident happened on August 12, 2013. Each month when the twelfth rolled around I would think about everyone I had lost, not just Andrew but also my parents and in-laws, friends, and

grandparents. My mind was set on my losses rather than on the gifts God had given me in Christ. Everywhere I went I thought about my pain and loss, so that is also what I talked about.

In July, eleven months after The Accident, I decided to stop that day from being the bad one of every month. I decided to be grateful. I began to write "Twelve Things I Am Grateful for on the 12th" of each month. I began to focus on all the wonderful things in my life instead of my loss. It was hard at first, but with practice, over time, I began to look forward to writing my "Gratitude List" each month. Looking for things to be grateful for became a habit. Just as it did for Lois (Lesson 4) when she chose to rejoice in each day the Lord made, choosing gratitude helped me heal and find joy again. I still miss those who died, but their memory brings me more joy than sorrow.

[Ron] Sometimes it seems impossible to deal with my selfishness, resentment, fear, and anger. These reared their ugly heads after we lost Andrew. Humility seemed beyond possibility. But I was able to practice gratitude. I have seen that doing this opens my heart to rescue by my loving Father. "Thank you Lord, please help me, thank you Lord," is a path to peace and humility.

Choosing Gratitude

Read the following passages about giving thanks. Circle the key words *thanks, thanksgiving, joy,* and *rejoice*. Note what you learn about gratitude and giving thanks. (Remember to add to your *Journal* page "What I Learned About God.")

Gratitude and Giving Thanks

PSALM 136:1

¹*Give thanks to the LORD, for he is good, for his steadfast love endures forever.*

David was suffering when he wrote this Psalm. He was surrounded by enemies, yet he praised God. What is the result of praise according to verses 31 and 32?

PSALM 69:29-32

29 But I am afflicted and in pain; let your salvation, O God, set me on high! 30 I will praise the name of God with a song; I will magnify him with thanksgiving. 31 This will please the LORD more than an ox or a bull with horns and hoofs. 32 When the humble see it they will be glad; you who seek God, let your hearts revive.

What does Paul command in these verses?

1 THESSALONIANS 5:16-18

16 Rejoice always, 17 pray without ceasing, 18 give thanks in all circumstances; for this is the will of God in Christ Jesus for you.

Why are we to do these things according to verse 18?

What do we learn about the qualities of the new body we receive?

1 CORINTHIANS 15:54-58

54 When the perishable puts on the imperishable, and the mortal puts on immortality, then shall come to pass the saying that is written: "Death is swallowed up in victory." 55 "O death, where is your victory? O death, where is your sting?" 56 The sting of death is sin, and the power of sin is the law. 57 But thanks be to God, who gives us the victory through our Lord Jesus Christ. 58 Therefore, my beloved brothers, be steadfast, immovable, always abounding in the work of the Lord, knowing that in the Lord your labor is not in vain.

According to verse 57 what has God done for us?

What should we do according to verse 58?

How does Habakkuk plan to respond to bad things?

What does he say about God in verse 19?

HABAKKUK 3:17-19

17 Though the fig tree should not blossom, nor fruit be on the vines, the produce of the olive fail and the fields yield no food, the flock be cut off from the fold and there be no herd in the stalls, 18 yet I will rejoice in the Lord; I will take joy in the God of my salvation. 19 God, the Lord, is my strength; he makes my feet like the deer's; he makes me tread on my high places.

You looked in-depth at this passage in the last lesson, but review is always good. List all the good qualities we're to "put on."

Good Qualities

COLOSSIANS 3:12-17

12 Put on then, as God's chosen ones, holy and beloved, compassionate hearts, kindness, humility, meekness, and patience, 13 bearing with one another and, if one has a complaint against another, forgiving each other; as the Lord has forgiven you, so you also must forgive. 14 And above all these put on love, which binds everything together in perfect harmony. 15 And let the peace of Christ rule in your hearts, to which indeed you were called in one body. And be thankful. 16 Let the word of Christ dwell in you richly, teaching and admonishing one another in all wisdom, singing psalms and hymns and spiritual songs, with thankfulness in your hearts to God. 17 And whatever you do, in word or deed, do everything in the name of the Lord Jesus, giving thanks to God the Father through him.

What does this passage teach about giving thanks?

Read Psalm 107:1-3 and underline any reference to the *Lord*. Circle the word *redeemed*.

Who is to give thanks?

PSALM 107:1-9, 43

Why?

What did "some" eventually do when they were hungry and thirsty?

What was the result?

List what the Lord did for His redeemed people.

*[1] Oh give thanks to the L*ORD*, for he is good, for his steadfast love endures forever! [2] Let the redeemed of the L*ORD *say so, whom he has redeemed from trouble [3] and gathered in from the lands, from the east and from the west, from the north and from the south. [4] Some wandered in desert wastes, finding no way to a city to dwell in; [5] hungry and thirsty, their soul fainted within them. [6] Then they cried to the L*ORD *in their trouble, and he delivered them from their distress. [7] He led them by a straight way till they reached a city to dwell in. [8] Let them thank the L*ORD *for his steadfast love, for his wondrous works to the children of man! [9] For he satisfies the longing soul, and the hungry soul he fills with good things.*

*[43] Whoever is wise, let him attend to these things; let them consider the steadfast love of the L*ORD*.*

Beloved, it may not seem as though the Lord has redeemed you from trouble as you go through grief. Are you willing to trust Him? Are you willing to cry out to Him? Are you willing to let Him do a transforming work in you? According to this passage, what will result if you do?

Look back at verses 1, 2, and 43. Why can we give thanks in everything?

The first chapter of James sheds light on why we can rejoice when we're going through trials. Read James 1:2-4.

What results from the testing of your faith?

JAMES 1:2-4

[2] *Count it all joy, my brothers, when you meet trials of various kinds, [3] for you know that the testing of your faith produces steadfastness. [4] And let steadfastness have its full effect, that you may be perfect and complete, lacking in nothing.*

If you have time, read the rest of James 1. James is a wonderful resource for us as we try to live in Christ through suffering and grief. We will study more from this book in a later lesson.

Psalm 107 tells us to give thanks because the Lord is good. We are told in Thessalonians that rejoicing, praying and giving thanks is the will of God for us. Colossians tells us to be thankful and let the word of God dwell in our hearts. James tells us the testing of our faith produces steadfastness which in turn helps us become perfect (mature) and complete, lacking nothing.

We are not told to rejoice or be happy because of our loss, but we are to rejoice because God loves us! He has redeemed us! He is doing a transforming work in us even as we grieve.

Rejoicing in what God has done for us in Christ is also a great way to stop the dark thoughts! When we think of all these wonderful things and give thanks to the Lord, when we dwell in Him and He in us, we're not dwelling on our loss. When Ron and I began to have an attitude of gratitude rather than constantly dwelling on our loss, we began to find joy and peace again!

Just Journaling

*Have you found yourself bitter about your loss rather than grateful about what you **had, have,** and **will have in Christ?** Do you think you can begin to rejoice in God? Can you rejoice because of what Jesus did for you? Write what you're thinking and feeling after studying these passages.*

Gratitude Lists

We have to work to change our thoughts. We must practice thankfulness for it to become a part of our daily lives.

How are you doing in this area? Do you thank God for the gifts He has given you? Do you share with others the wonderful things He has done for you?

A *Gratitude List* can help us change what we think about. When we change our thoughts to set our mind on things of the Spirit and the wonderful things we have in our life, we have other things to talk about with our friends and family besides death, grief, and sorrow. As we study and apply the Word of God in our lives we not only begin to heal, we also begin to do the next right thing. We begin to care for and serve others as well.

One way to make a monthly *Gratitude List* is to pick a special date, for example your loved one's birthdate. Make a list of things to be grateful for on that date each month like Kathleen's "Twelve Things I am grateful for on the 12th."

You can also make an annual *Gratitude List*. From a grief group we're part of, a mom posted three things she was grateful for on the anniversary of her child's death:

1. Something I am grateful for *from* my child's *life*

2. Something I am grateful for *in* my child's *death*

3. Something I am grateful for *since* my child's *death*

[Kathleen] Here are three things I wrote about my mother-in-law Rita:

<u>*Something I am grateful for from Rita's life*</u>*: I'm glad I got to be her daughter-in law for twenty-eight years. She taught me how to be a better wife and mom. And she taught how to love others . . . by her example.*

<u>*Something I am grateful for in Rita's death*</u>*: I'm grateful that I was able to help care for her in her home the last five weeks of her life , along with Ron, my family, and three brothers-in-law and their wives. It was an honor to care for this godly woman. The burden was made lighter for all of us by David and Nancy who were there to help almost daily.*

<u>*Something I am grateful for since Rita's death*</u>*: I'm grateful for the legacy she left in her four amazing sons. She taught them well how to love God and their families. She also showed them that when they are not perfect, when they sin, they will find forgiveness in Jesus Christ. I am privileged to be married to one of Rita's sons.*

One young lady we know began a *Daily Thankful List* the week of The Accident. She knew all five of the young people killed that night. She had worked with them all summer and loved them. She started her list in a small notebook she carries with her. Each day she writes at least one thing she's thankful for. In the last three years she has added thousands of things to her *Daily Thankful List!* Being grateful to God for His gifts in her life has helped her heal from the trauma of losing five friends in one night.

Can you think of things you're grateful for? Why not start your own *Gratitude List* and *Daily Thankful List?* Try writing three things you are grateful for from the life and death of the ones you have lost. Be sure to include something you are grateful for since your loss.

Just as in the last lesson we made a list of things to think about—things that are true, noble, right, pure, lovely, commendable, excellent and praiseworthy—make a list of things in your life today that bring you joy, things you are grateful for. It doesn't need to be a long list; you can start with just a few things and add to it over time. This list is a tool to turn to in the dark times. It will remind you of the good things in your life. Practicing gratitude will help you find healing, hope, peace, and joy even during suffering.

Just Journaling

In your Journal, begin to list things you're grateful for today. If you're making your own Journal, label pages for a list of what you are grateful for and add to your list often.

If you're using our companion Journal, you'll find space for your "Gratitude List" as well as space to complete your "Gratitude List (Annual)."

Knowing What God Has Done for You

Knowing the Giver can help us be thankful in all things. This is one reason why we asked you to make a list of what you learned about God in this study. It also helps to have a list of what He has done for you including gifts He has given you. Knowing who God is and who we are in Christ helps us walk through life with confidence in Him. When we have confidence in Him and learn to trust Him, we find healing, hope, peace, and joy.

For the rest of this lesson we're going to study who we are in Christ and what God has done for us as well as a few promises of what He will do.

Read each passage and double-underline references to *in Christ*. Mark key words. Note what you learn about **God** and **you in Christ**.

God / Me in Christ

IIn whose image were you made?

Who are you in Christ?

GENESIS 1:26

²⁶ *Then God said, "Let us make man in our image, after our likeness. And let them have dominion over the fish of the sea and over the birds of the heavens and over the livestock and over all the earth and over every creeping thing that creeps on the earth."*

GALATIANS 3:25-29

²⁵ *But now that faith has come, we are no longer under a guardian,* ²⁶ *for in Christ Jesus you are all sons of God, through faith.* ²⁷ *For as many of you as were baptized into Christ have put on Christ.* ²⁸ *There is neither Jew nor Greek, there is neither slave nor free, there is no male and female, for you are all one*

God / Me in Christ

When were you chosen?

For what?

What has he blessed you with in the beloved?

What have you gained through his blood?

What happened when you believed in Him?

What did Jesus preach?

What do we have through Him?

in Christ Jesus. ²⁹ And if you are Christ's, then you are Abraham's offspring, heirs according to promise.

EPHESIANS 1:4-7, 11-13

⁴ even as he chose us in him before the foundation of the world, that we should be holy and blameless before him. In love ⁵ he predestined us for adoption to himself as sons through Jesus Christ, according to the purpose of his will, ⁶ to the praise of his glorious grace, with which he has blessed us in the Beloved. ⁷ In him we have redemption through his blood, the forgiveness of our trespasses, according to the riches of his grace,

¹¹ In him we have obtained an inheritance, having been predestined according to the purpose of him who works all things according to the counsel of his will, ¹² so that we who were the first to hope in Christ might be to the praise of his glory. ¹³ In him you also, when you heard the word of truth, the gospel of your salvation, and believed in him, were sealed with the promised Holy Spirit,

EPHESIANS 2:17-18

¹⁷ And he came and preached peace to you who were far off and peace to those who werenear. ¹⁸ For through him we both have access in one Spirit to the Father.

God / Me in Christ

According to this passage, what will we experience as children of God?

What do you learn from verses 29-30 about every child of God?

What do you learn about your body from this passage?

What do you learn about being in Christ in verse 17?

What do you learn about reconciliation in verses 18-19?

ROMANS 8:16-17, 29-30

16 The Spirit himself bears witness with our spirit that we are children of God, 17 and if children, then heirs—heirs of God and fellow heirs with Christ, provided we suffer with him in order that we may also be glorified with him.

29 For those whom he foreknew he also predestined to be conformed to the image of his Son, in order that he might be the firstborn among many brothers. 30 And those whom he predestined he also called, and those whom he called he also justified, and those whom he justified he also glorified.

1 CORINTHIANS 6:19-20

19 Or do you not know that your body is a temple of the Holy Spirit within you, whom you have from God? You are not your own, 20 for you were bought with a price. So glorify God in your body.

2 CORINTHIANS 5:17-21

17 Therefore, if anyone is in Christ, he is a new creation. The old has passed away; behold, the new has come. 18 All this is from God, who through Christ reconciled us to himself and gave us the ministry of reconciliation; 19 that is, in Christ God was reconciling the world to himself, not counting their trespasses against them, and entrusting to us the message of reconciliation.

God / Me in Christ

What does God call us in verse 20?

What do you become in Him according to verse 21?

Why did God send His Son into the world?

How does God describe you in this passage?

What have you been set free from?

What are you now a slave of?

[20] *Therefore, we are ambassadors for Christ, God making his appeal through us. We implore you on behalf of Christ, be reconciled to God.* *[21]* *For our sake he made him to be sin who knew no sin, so that in him we might become the righteousness of God.*

JOHN 3:16-17

[16] *For God so loved the world that he gave his one and only Son, that whoever believes in him shall not perish but have eternal life.* *[17]* *For God did not send his Son into the world to condemn the world, but to save the world through him.*

1 PETER 2:9-10

[9] *But you are a chosen race, a royal priesthood, a holy nation, a people for his own possession, that you may proclaim the excellencies of him who called you out of darkness into his marvelous light.* *[10]* *Once you were not a people, but now you are God's people; once you had not received mercy, but now you have received mercy.*

ROMANS 6:17-18

[17] *But thanks be to God, that you who were once slaves of sin have become obedient from the heart to the standard of teaching to which you were committed,* *[18]* *and, having been set free from sin, have become slaves of righteousness.*

God / Me in Christ

What has God given us?

Where is our citizenship?

What will Christ Jesus do when He returns according to this passage?

What does this passage tell you about your abilities?

What does this passage tell you about how you were formed?

What is written in God's book?

2 TIMOTHY 1:7

7 for God gave us a spirit not of fear but of power and love and self-control.

PHILIPPIANS 3:20-21

20 But our citizenship is in heaven, and from it we await a Savior, the Lord Jesus Christ, 21 who will transform our lowly body to be like his glorious body, by the power that enables him even to subject all things to himself.

PHILIPPIANS 4:13

13 I can do all things through him who strengthens me.

PSALM 139:16

16 Your eyes saw my unformed substance; in your book were written, every one of them, the days that were formed for me, when as yet there was none of them.

Beloved, aren't these things worthy of gratitude? Reading through all these passages and learning about who you are in Christ will make you grateful to God! Take time now to thank Him for all He has done for you.

Just Journaling

Be sure to add to your list of "What I Learned About God" (in the back of the Companion Journal). Then create a list of "Who I Am in Christ" in your Healing in Grief Journal. Include God's promises to those in Him. As you study God's Word add to these lists. When you are feeling low or unworthy, turn to them and remind yourself of who you are in Christ.

LESSON 12

How Should We React When Others Hurt Us?

. . . pray for those who abuse you (Luke 6:28b).

[Ron] *Many of our friends and acquaintances expressed their condolences when Andrew was killed. A small number were, frankly, unhelpful. "They mean well," someone would comment, but I had to think, if they really meant well, wouldn't they have stopped and thought a little more before saying something so insensitive or just plain stupid? The fact is, people were uncomfortable, fearful, sad, upset, and concerned about us but some were generally not in a position to articulate God's light and life to us. I learned that a "a word fitly spoken" (Proverbs 25:11) is precious because it is rare. I realized that if I could learn to speak those kind words at the right time, this would be a remarkably exceptional gift to someone. I also learned to give other people a break when they said something less than remarkably exceptional.*

There were times when visitors tried to share their comfort but actually they were desperate for comfort themselves. In one instance I thought, "It's OK if you don't comfort me, but could you stop your tearful rant about the injustice of my son's untimely death . . . or at least leave my house to do it?" Other friends were incredibly helpful, usually in simple ways. One said he'd heard about the loss of our son, then without pausing told us he had come to understand what a remarkable young man Andrew was. That was very encouraging. He simply focused on saying something nice about our son's life instead of saying he was very sorry about Andrew's death but leaving me to respond in a way that wouldn't help either of us.

Several friends in the Air Force at a local base contacted me. A couple of them were encouraging with striking and gentle strength. They called or texted and briefly said they were praying for me. I knew they were no strangers to violent death, yet they were living the life of Christ. They gently persisted in following up with me, and still do. They helped me believe we would get through this.

Whenever we spend time with parents who have lost children or others who are grieving, someone brings up the subject of hurtful or offensive things others have said to them in their grief. It's natural to make a mental list of the offensive and theologically inaccurate things others have said to us. It's natural to be hurt by offensive things people say and to harbor anger and bitterness.

People generally do not know what to say to grieving people. They mean well; they try to comfort. But being flawed humans they say wrong things or nothing at all which can hurt just as much. It's easy to spend time thinking and talking about all the ways we have been wronged during our grief.

In the last two lessons we looked at different ways to change our thoughts away from loss and sorrow. We looked at choosing to set our minds on things of the Spirit and being grateful for God's gifts in our lives. We can also choose to forgive offenses and not spend time talking about or thinking of the wrong things well-meaning people said to us.

Today, instead of thinking of the offensive things well-meaning people said or did, try to make a list of kind things people have done for you during your grief—meals, cards, services. Be specific. For example, one friend came to walk with Kathleen twice each week for months after The Accident. Getting outside, exercising, and having a friend to talk with helped her begin to heal.

Just Journaling

Write at the top of a page in your Healing in Grief Journal "Kind Things People Did and Said." Add at least five things to this list today. Pray and thank God for them and for what they did. Add to this list whenever someone does something kind for you.

Did you have a hard time making this list? Was it hard for you to think of kind things people did for you in your grief? If so, are you harboring resentment against people who hurt you? Resentment makes it hard to think of good things in our lives.

Sometimes family members around us are also grieving. In their pain they lash out intentionally and hurt us, those they love. In our pain we may hurt those closest to us too. In this lesson we're going to look at how we should react when someone hurts us.

How should we react when others unintentionally or intentionally offend us with their words and/or actions?

Read the following verses. Mark *forgive* and *forgiveness*. Underline instructions regarding how we should behave towards others. Note what you learn.

Then, in the left column, write how you are doing obeying each instruction. Are you doing well at each? Or do you need to work on something? Be honest. If you need to work on some of these, ask the Holy Spirit to help you.

How Am I Doing?

MATTHEW 6:14-15
¹⁴ *For if you forgive others their trespasses, your heavenly Father will also forgive you,* ¹⁵ *but if you do not forgive others their trespasses, neither will your Father forgive your trespasses.*

EPHESIANS 4:1-3
¹ *I therefore, a prisoner for the Lord, urge you to walk in a manner worthy of the calling to which you have been called,* ² *with all humility and gentleness, with patience, bearing with one another in love,* ³ *eager to maintain the unity of the Spirit in the bond of peace.*

MATTHEW 18:15, 21-22
¹⁵ *If your brother sins against you, go and tell him his fault, between you and him alone. If he listens to you, you have gained your brother.*

²¹ *Then Peter came up and said to him, "Lord, how often will my brother sin against me, and I forgive him? As many as seven times?"* ²² *Jesus said to him, "I do not say to you seven times, but seventy-seven times.*

How Am I Doing?

LUKE 6:31-33, 36

[31] And as you wish that others would do to you, do so to them. [32] "If you love those who love you, what benefit is that to you? For even sinners love those who love them. [33] And if you do good to those who do good to you, what benefit is that to you? For even sinners do the same

[36] Be merciful, even as your Father is merciful.

ROMANS 12:14-18

[14] Bless those who persecute you; bless and do not curse them. [15] Rejoice with those who rejoice, weep with those who weep. [16] Live in harmony with one another. Do not be haughty, but associate with the lowly. Never be wise in your own sight. [17] Repay no one evil for evil, but give thought to do what is honorable in the sight of all. [18] If possible, so far as it depends on you, live peaceably with all.

[20] To the contrary, "if your enemy is hungry, feed him; if he is thirsty, give him something to drink; for by so doing you will heap burning coals on his head." [21] Do not be overcome by evil, but overcome evil with good.

It's not easy to be merciful when we're hurting. Often we're inwardly-focused when we're grieving and don't want to be merciful to others! We do want them to be merciful to us! We may want to hurt them if they hurt us. But Jesus tells us to be merciful. Jesus tells us to forgive.

Read the following passages and underline any instructions regarding how we should respond to others when they say things that hurt you. Write what you learn.

How to Respond	
	TITUS 3:2
	[2] to speak evil of no one, to avoid quarreling, to be gentle, and to show perfect courtesy toward all people.
	2 TIMOTHY 2:24-25
	[24] And the Lord's servant must not be quarrelsome but kind to everyone, able to teach, patiently enduring evil, [25] correcting his opponents with gentleness. God may perhaps grant them repentance leading to a knowledge of the truth
	PROVERBS 15:1
	[1] A soft answer turns away wrath, but a harsh word stirs up anger.
	JAMES 1:19-21
	[19] Know this, my beloved brothers: let every person be quick to hear, slow to speak, slow to anger; [20] for the anger of man does not produce the righteousness of God. [21] Therefore put away all filthiness and rampant wickedness and receive with meekness the implanted word, which is able to save your souls.

Sometimes when we're already wounded we naturally lash out at those who have offended us. We may even argue with people who are trying to help and love us through our grief. When someone says something hurtful or something we believe is wrong, should we hurt them back or argue with them?

There are many verses throughout Scripture that command us to forgive others who have hurt us. It is not an option! It's also not something we do because we feel like it. When you're grieving badly you may not want to forgive; you may not feel like forgiving.

But with God's help you can be gracious toward those who say hurtful things to you in your grief. They're trying to help you but often they do it in flawed ways. They're trying to love you and show you they care. They may not do it well, but they *are* trying.

Let's go back to a question we asked at the beginning of this lesson: are you harboring resentment against someone who hurt you in the midst of your grief? Did they offend you with something they said or did, or both? Did you show them mercy? If not, now's a good time to talk to God about the situation. Ask Him to give you mercy to those around you.

> *[Kathleen] Recently during a Bible Study Program, I realized that I was harboring resentment and unforgiveness towards a family member who had deeply hurt me in the early months of my grief. She was hurting as well because of her loss and lashed out at me many times. I wrote in my notebook a prayer. I confessed my anger, told God that I was choosing to obey Him and forgive her, and asked Him to help me walk that out. I signed and dated that prayer. Our relationship has been much better since I repented and forgave her.*

Do you need to forgive someone today? Ask God to help you forgive him or her. Write your intention to forgive in a brief prayer here. Sign and date it like Kathleen. Then . . . don't resurrect bitterness!

Just Journaling

When you lose a loved one, remember that others, too, have lost a child, a parent, a friend, a sibling. They may still be grieving and need comfort and love themselves. Maybe it will help you to write out your thoughts in your Journal. Include a summary of what you learned about forgiveness.

Is there someone you need to forgive? Pray and talk to God about it. Forgive him or her and ask Him to help you walk that out. Write your thoughts about the situation in light of the passages you've studied.

Maybe you can write the person a letter, extending your forgiveness if he or she sinned against you. You may not need to send it at all, but writing it out will help you.

Repenting of Bad Behavior

Have you grown tired of the wrong things people say as they try to comfort you? Have you retaliated with sarcasm or insults? Have you lashed out at a family member during your grief? Have you argued with others or treated them badly? Have you hurt others with your words or deeds due to your grief or because they hurt you? Have you sinned and blamed your sin on your grief?

We've heard grieving people say things like "This is just how it is. I'm hurting and everyone else can deal with it!" My friend, in our grief we will find ourselves thinking, saying, and doing ugly things. At times we'll think we can't help ourselves so we're acquitted. But if we think of these things as our rights (justified and acceptable) we're foolishly mistaken. This is, in effect, embracing and practicing sin rather than recognizing it, confessing it to God, then repenting of it as He energizes (Colossians 1:29) us to do this.

Let's look at what Scripture tells us to do when we sin against someone. But first, let's look at why we behave a certain way. Why do we sometimes get angry or yell at those we love? Is grief the reason we lash out at those around us?

This may not be comfortable. You may learn some things that cause you to think differently about your behavior and excuses. Beloved, the truth is not always easy, but it will set you free.

Read James 1:13-15. Circle the word *tempted*. Note what you learn from each passage.

Temptation	**JAMES 1:13-15**
List who or what tempts us into sin.	*13 Let no one say when he is tempted, "I am being tempted by God," for God cannot be tempted with evil, and he himself tempts no one. 14 But each person is tempted when he is lured and enticed by his own desire. 15 Then desire when it has conceived gives birth to sin, and sin when it is fully grown brings forth death.*
What chain of events does James reveal?	
What is the end result of sin?	

Now read Romans 3:10-18 and answer the questions below.

Are any of us without sin? Who is righteous?

What is our nature according to these verses and so how do we *naturally* speak?

ROMANS 3:10-18

[10] *"None is righteous, no, not one;* [11] *no one understands; no one seeks for God.* [12] *All have turned aside; together they have become worthless; no one does good, not even one."* [13] *"Their throat is an open grave; they use their tongues to deceive." "The venom of asps is under their lips."* [14] *"Their mouth is full of curses and bitterness."* [15] *"Their feet are swift to shed blood;* [16] *in their paths are ruin and misery,* [17] *and the way of peace they have not known."* [18] *"There is no fear of God before their eyes."*

Read James 4:1-3. Underline *quarrels* and *fights*.

List what causes quarrels and fights.

JAMES 4:1-3

[1] *What causes quarrels and what causes fights among you? Is it not this, that your passions are at war within you?* [2] *You desire and do not have, so you murder. You covet and cannot obtain, so you fight and quarrel. You do not have, because you do not ask.* [3] *You ask and do not receive, because you ask wrongly, to spend it on your passions.*

Ouch! James 1 says our desires lead us to sin. James 3 says quarrels and fights are caused by our passions. We cannot have what we want, so we quarrel and fight. Romans 3 tells us that no one is righteous, that we all have turned aside. We use our tongues to deceive, and our mouths are full of curses and bitterness. Ouch, again!

According to these scriptures is grief the true reason we act in ugly ways? Does grief cause sin? Write down your thoughts.

Do these verses describe you? We know many grieving parents who want their children back alive on earth. Many of us would love to have our parents back with us as we raise our children. We can't have these things. Our loved ones are away from their bodies and at home with the Lord. Maybe you're are missing them and wish you could spend just five more minutes with them.

We are hurting, but do we have to let unfulfilled desire cause us to sin? Is there a way for us to not sin in our grief and pain?

Read the following scriptures, mark key words, and write what you learn.

Instructions

1 CORINTHIANS 10:13

13 No temptation has overtaken you that is not common to man. God is faithful, and he will not let you be tempted beyond your ability, but with the temptation he will also provide the way of escape, that you may be able to endure it.

JAMES 4:6-8, 10

6 But he gives more grace. Therefore it says, "God opposes the proud, but gives grace to the humble." 7 Submit yourselves therefore to God. Resist the devil, and he will flee from you. 8 Draw near to God, and he will draw near to you.

10 Humble yourselves before the Lord, and he will exalt you.

HEBREWS 2:14-18

Whose power did Jesus destroy according to this passage?

14 Since therefore the children share in flesh and blood, he himself likewise partook of the same things, that through death he might destroy the one who has the power of death, that is, the devil, 15 and deliver all those who through fear of death were subject to lifelong slavery. 16 For surely it is not angels that he helps, but he helps

Who does He help and who does He not help?

What qualifies Him to help?

> the offspring of Abraham. [17] Therefore he had to be made like his brothers in every respect, so that he might become a merciful and faithful high priest in the service of God, to make propitiation for the sins of the people. [18] For because he himself has suffered when tempted, he is able to help those who are being tempted.

Does grief give us the right to be angry and hurtful to others? Is it *only* because we are in pain that we lash out at those around us? Are conflicts always someone else's fault? Summarize what you learned.

None of us is perfect. We all mess up. In our grief we sin and hurt others. What should you do when you do this? If you offend family or friends when you're grieving, what can you do to reconcile the relationship?

Read the following passages, underline any instructions, and note what you learn.

Instructions

MATTHEW 5:23-24

> [23] So if you are offering your gift at the altar and there remember that your brother has something against you, [24] leave your gift there before the altar and go. First be reconciled to your brother, and then come and offer your gift.

Instructions	**JAMES 5:16**
	[16] *Therefore, confess your sins to one another and pray for one another, that you may be healed. The prayer of a righteous person has great power as it is working.*
What's the danger of denying that we sin?	**1 JOHN 1:8-9**
	[8] *If we say we have no sin, we deceive ourselves, and the truth is not in us.* [9] *If we confess our sins, he is faithful and just to forgive us our sins and to cleanse us from all unrighteousness.*
What does God do when we confess our sins and on what basis?	

Whatever Makes You Feel Better?

Some friends may tell you, "It's your grief. Do whatever makes you feel better." This advice is only as good as the "whatever." If the "whatever" is turning to the Lord and His Word, it's good.

When we're physically ill we need wise counsel from a physician, not *whatever feels right* which can actually make us worse in the long-run. If you have a severe wound on your leg it may *feel better* to leave it alone than to endure the pain of having it cleaned out and stitched up. But if you don't care for it properly, the wound will get infected and . . . you could lose your leg and possibly your life.

Similarly, when our heart and emotions are wounded, we should seek the counsel of the Great Physician and apply His wisdom to our situation rather than doing what "makes us feel better" in the moment. Often what makes us feel better today is only a temporary fix. We find that we wake up the next day with the same pain or worse. We need the true healing which comes from seeking God, studying His Word, and applying the truth in our lives.

[Kathleen] As I wrote in a previous lesson, I came to realize that I was talking about The Accident more than Ron was. I also realized that grief, death, and loss were all I talked about some days because they were all I thought about. I know Ron got tired of hearing me talk about our loss and my grief. Our adult children actually told me they were tired of hearing about it. I realized I was being selfish; I was not caring about their loss and pain. I didn't care about their needs or interests. My talking about my pain and my grief did not help them heal in their grief. And, truth be told, thinking, talking, and writing only about my pain was not helping me heal either.

I knew that I needed to change what I was thinking about. I needed to change what I was talking about with friends and family. I needed to think about other things so I could talk about other things. I also needed to begin to listen to my family and friends, to hear about their lives and struggles and to care about their interests, not about my own only. So I began to work on listening to others rather than talking all the time. I worked on caring for the interests and needs of those around me.

You may have had friends or family express that they did not want to hear or read about your loss. They may have told you they don't want to hear about the person you lost. We know it hurts when others say things like that. We want to talk about our loved one, even if makes others uncomfortable.

It hurts when someone tells us we're dominating conversations with our grief, but we need to ask ourselves if there is any truth to their allegation. We need to ask ourselves, "Am I dominating conversations? Do I post on social media about grief too much? Do I talk about it too much in Sunday School, Small Group, or Bible Study? Do I talk about death too much?" For us, sometimes the answers to these questions were "Yes!" Sometimes we did selfishly ignore the needs of others.

What can we do about this? We can seek God, study what Scripture says about how to speak to and treat others, and then apply what we learn. Here are a few scriptures that can help you change your behavior. Though some of them are hard and may make you uncomfortable, studying and applying them to your life will help you. They are from the Word of God. Are you willing to let God transform you through the renewing of your mind as you study these hard things? We pray that you are.

Let's look at a few passages about relationships. Read the following and underline instructions. Mark any key words including *selfish, humility,* and references to *speech*. Note what you learn about how to treat others. Make a list of what you learn about speech.

How To Treat Others

PHILIPPIANS 2:1-4

^{1} So if there is any encouragement in Christ, any comfort from love, any participation in the Spirit, any affection and sympathy, ^{2} complete my joy by being of the same mind, having the same love, being in full accord and of one mind. ^{3} Do nothing from selfish ambition or conceit, but in humility count others more significant than yourselves. ^{4} Let each of you look not only to his own interests, but also to the interests of others.

Speech

PROVERBS 10:17-19

^{17} Whoever heeds instruction is on the path to life, but he who rejects reproof leads others astray. ^{18} The one who conceals hatred has lying lips, and whoever utters slander is a fool. ^{19} When words are many, transgression is not lacking, but whoever restrains his lips is prudent.

Speech

EPHESIANS 4:25-32

^{25} Therefore, having put away falsehood, let each one of you speak the truth with his neighbor, for we are members one of another. ^{26} Be angry and do not sin; do not let the sun go down on your anger, ^{27} and give no opportunity to the devil. ^{28} Let the thief no longer steal, but rather let him labor, doing honest

How To Treat Others

work with his own hands, so that he may have something to share with anyone in need. [29] Let no corrupting talk come out of your mouths, but only such as is good for building up, as fits the occasion, that it may give grace to those who hear. [30] And do not grieve the Holy Spirit of God, by whom you were sealed for the day of redemption. [31] Let all bitterness and wrath and anger and clamor and slander be put away from you, along with all malice. [32] Be kind to one another, tenderhearted, forgiving one another, as God in Christ forgave you.

Speech

EPHESIANS 5:18-21

[18] And do not get drunk with wine, for that is debauchery, but be filled with the Spirit, [19] addressing one another in psalms and hymns and spiritual songs, singing and making melody to the Lord with your heart, [20] giving thanks always and for everything to God the Father in the name of our Lord Jesus Christ, [21] submitting to one another out of reverence for Christ.

Speech

ROMANS 12:14-18

[14] Bless those who persecute you; bless and do not curse them. [15] Rejoice with those who rejoice, weep with those who weep. [16] Live in harmony with one another. Do not be haughty, but associate with the lowly. Never be wise in your own sight. [17] Repay no one evil for evil, but give thought to do what is honorable in the sight of all. [18] If possible, so far as it depends on you, live peaceably with all.

How To Treat Others

Summarize what you learned about speech.

To review, list the instructions on how to treat others you found in these passages.

Did any of these passages give exceptions to the instructions? Did any of them qualify with "except when you're grieving"?

As we grieve we must apply the Word of God in our lives. We don't get a "pass" to sit and think about dark things and be selfishly rude to others just because we're hurting. We must guard our thoughts, tongues, and other actions. We must care for the interests of others. We must apply truth in our lives as we grieve in order to find healing, hope, peace, and joy.

Please know that we are not saying you should jump back into volunteering at church or leading Bible studies the day after a funeral. We are not saying you should care for others at the expense of your own health. You need to care for your own health and take time to mourn. You need time to heal in your grief. But, as we learned in Lesson 2, time spent doing the wrong things will harm rather than heal us. If we spend months or years thinking and talking only about death, sorrow, and grief and ruminating about resentments, we will not find hope, joy, peace, and healing.

We must set our minds on things above. We must choose to be thankful for the gifts God has given us rather than thinking and talking only about the things we have lost. We must forgive those who hurt us and repent of our sin. We must care for others, bear their burdens, serve Christ by serving them.

Just Journaling

In your Journal, summarize what you learned about how to speak to and treat others.

Ask God to show you to what extent you're living up to these commands we studied in this lesson. Write down the things He shows you that you need to change. Confess your sin to Him and ask Him to forgive you.

This next step is hard, but worth doing! Make a list of people you have sinned against. Ask God to give you opportunities to ask for their forgiveness and be reconciled to them.

LESSON 13

Did Someone Cause the Death of Your Loved One?

In an earlier lesson we looked at God's sovereignty and Scripture passages that say He numbers our days. We also saw that people sometimes act in ways that result in the death of another person. Most of these are not intentional. Still, many of us may blame them for the death of our loved one.

Our son was killed in a car wreck. A friend of his was the designated driver for the trip but unknown to the passengers he was drunk and ran a stop sign. He should not have been behind the wheel of a car. A large truck going very fast struck the car our son was riding in and five beautiful young people including the driver and our son, died that night.

Kathleen wrote the following on her blog just a couple of months after The Accident:

Amazingly, I have never been mad at the driver.

The day we found out about The Accident, Ron and I talked to each other about how Andrew's life was complete. It was completed the moment he died and in other ways it was complete every day—he lived life to the fullest, doing what he loved and doing it well. He had launched into adulthood well. He knew Jesus. What more could a parent ask for?

We were sad and disappointed, but not angry.

I've been angry at times over the past couple of months but not at a person; it's more like anger at the whole situation. But each time anger over losing Andrew tries to creep into my mind, Scripture quickly pops into my head, reminding me of truth. The Holy Spirit gently and kindly reminds me of truth.

Fleeting feelings of anger is not sin. But if we grasp hold of anger, dwell on it, and justify it as "our right" we are on very dangerous ground. Recall that Jesus compared unjustifiable anger to murder and made it clear that it would result in grave consequences (Matthew 5:21-22).

I could park myself there and go about life filled with anger, rage, and resentment which would make me hateful and hurtful to others. And I would answer to the Lord for it.

I am so grateful for all the time I have spent in the Word over the years. I know truth and truth has set me free—free <u>from</u> anger, bitterness, fear, regret, worry, and free <u>to</u> trust God even when I do not understand why He allowed this to happen.

We live in a broken and fallen world. Bad things happen but He still causes His sun to shine and His rain to fall on the just and the unjust. We serve a good and beautiful God!! And who can be angry about that?

Was someone else at fault in the death of your loved one? Maybe your loved one was murdered or died due to the errors of others. Do you think someone should have seen the depression of your loved one and stopped her from taking her life? Perhaps someone is actually responsible for the incident that caused the death of your child, sibling, parent, or other loved one.

Do you blame someone for the death that is causing you so much pain? What can we do about this? What do we do when another person has caused a death? Is it our place to get revenge? Is it okay to be angry? Do we have to forgive this person? Is forgiving the person or persons who caused the death the same as saying that what they did is okay? These are questions for which we can find answers in the Word of God.

When Actions Were Illegal

There are times when a person acts illegally and is responsible for someone's death. The law should be involved; those who commit crimes should be held accountable for them.

Read Romans 13:1-5 and note what you learn about judgment by "the governing authorities."

The Governing Authorities

ROMANS 13:1-5

[1] *Let every person be subject to the governing authorities. For there is no authority except from God, and those that exist have been instituted*

The Governing Authorities

Whose servant is the governing authority?

Whose wrath is carried out on the wrong-doer?

Taking verses 4 and 5 together, who should we not take vengeance on?

by God. ² *Therefore whoever resists the authorities resists what God has appointed, and those who resist will incur judgment. ³ For rulers are not a terror to good conduct, but to bad. Would you have no fear of the one who is in authority? Then do what is good, and you will receive his approval, ⁴ for he is God's servant for your good. But if you do wrong, be afraid, for he does not bear the sword in vain. For he is the servant of God, an avenger who carries out God's wrath on the wrongdoer. ⁵ Therefore one must be in subjection, not only to avoid God's wrath but also for the sake of conscience.*

Read Proverbs 21:15. What does it say about justice?

Justice

PROVERBS 21:15

¹⁵ *When justice is done, it is a joy to the righteous but terror to evildoers.*

If a person is legally responsible for your loved one's death, it's not your right and job to punish. This does not mean you shouldn't go to authorities or take the person to court to seek restitution. As Paul states, we should let the governing authorities do the job God has given them.

Before we move on, take time to think and write about what you just read. Are you tempted to take personal revenge or are you willing to let the law handle your case? Write what you're thinking.

Vengeance

Aside from justice under the law, what can we do when someone is to blame for a death? What do we do with our feelings of anger, rage, and desire for revenge? How do we handle them? Should those who caused the death pay some price for what they have done? Is it up to us to make them pay?

Read the following and circle the words *retribution, judge, judgment,* and *vengeance.* Note who judges evil and therefore who should *not* "repay." Write out what you learn about judgment and vengeance from these passages.

Who Judges

What kind of judgment characterizes God?

What does He consider just?

What will He do for the afflicted?

When will this happen?

How should we treat enemies and what general principle does God command?

2 THESSALONIANS 1:4-10

4 Therefore we ourselves boast about you in the churches of God for your steadfastness and faith in all your persecutions and in the afflictions that you are enduring. 5 This is evidence of the righteous judgment of God, that you may be considered worthy of the kingdom of God, for which you are also suffering— 6 since indeed God considers it just to repay with affliction those who afflict you, 7 and to grant relief to you who are afflicted as well as to us, when the Lord Jesus is revealed from heaven with his mighty angels 8 in flaming fire, inflicting vengeance on those who do not know God and on those who do not obey the gospel of our Lord Jesus. 9 They will suffer the punishment of eternal destruction, away from the presence of the Lord and from the glory of his might, 10 when he comes on that day to be glorified in his saints, and to be marveled at among all who have believed, because our testimony to you was believed.

Who Judges?

Who Repays?

Judgments and Vengeance

ROMANS 12:17-21.

17 Repay no one evil for evil, but give thought to do what is honorable in the sight of all. 18 If possible, so far as it depends on you, live peaceably with all. 19 Beloved, never avenge yourselves, but leave it to the wrath of God, for it is written, "Vengeance is mine, I will repay, says the Lord." 20 To the contrary, "if your enemy is hungry, feed him; if he is thirsty, give him something to drink; for by so doing you will heap burning coals on his head." 21 Do not be overcome by evil, but overcome evil with good.

Who Judges?

Who Repays?

DEUTERONOMY 32:35-36

35 Vengeance is mine, and recompense, for the time when their foot shall slip; for the day of their calamity is at hand, and their doom comes swiftly.' 36 For the LORD will vindicate his people and have compassion on his servants.

Who Judges?

Who Repays?

Judgments and Vengeance

PROVERBS 3:29-35

29 Do not plan evil against your neighbor, who dwells trustingly beside you. 30 Do not contend with a man for no reason, when he has done you no harm. 31 Do not envy a man of violence and do not choose any of his ways, 32 for the devious person is an abomination to the Lord, but the upright are in his confidence. 33 The LORD's curse is on the house of the wicked, but he blesses the dwelling of the righteous. 34 Toward the scorners he is scornful, but to the humble he gives favor. 35 The wise will inherit honor, but fools get disgrace.

What did you learn about how you are to treat others in this last passage from Proverbs? Make a list of all instructions.

According to these next two passages, is it okay to be a witness against your neighbor and if so, when?

PROVERBS 24:28-29

[28] *Be not a witness against your neighbor without cause, and do not deceive with your lips.* [29] *Do not say, "I will do to him as he has done to me; I will pay the man back for what he has done."*

JAMES 4:11-12

[11] *Do not speak evil against one another, brothers. The one who speaks against a brother or judges his brother, speaks evil against the law and judges the law. But if you judge the law, you are not a doer of the law but a judge.* [12] *There is only one lawgiver and judge, he who is able to save and to destroy. But who are you to judge your neighbor?*

Summarize what you learned from these passages about vengeance and how you are to act when someone has hurt you or someone you love.

Beloved, do we have authority to take vengeance? Who should we defer to?

Remember what you studied in Lesson 6? God has numbered our days; He controls life and death. God rules and reigns over all.

You may blame another person for a death and want to take vengeance. But that is not your place. Even if legal action is necessary, you must forgive.

You must figure out how you will respond to God in the midst of your pain and sorrow. Will you be transformed into the image of Christ willingly or not?

Just Journaling

Write what you learned about vengeance and how we should respond when others are at fault. Are you willing to trust God to judge?

Me? Forgive whom?

When we're wounded it's hard to forgive, yet we're told to do just that. Jesus did not say "Forgive everyone except those you blame for a death." Nor did He say "Forgive the slight but not the grave offenses." Our Lord told us to love our enemies as He did when He forgave those who were crucifying Him. He calls us to follow Him in loving and forgiving those who harm us. As a follower of Jesus we must forgive others just as God in Christ forgave us. Even grief caused by the actions of others is not an excuse for bitterness, resentment, or unforgiveness.

Forgiving does not mean you approve an action. Forgiveness does not make sin okay but it also does not mean you can't go to authorities for legal justice. You can forgive people and still let the legal system punish them for their crime. Hopefully this will keep them from repeating their offenses.

Forgiveness means you no longer position yourself as judge; you no longer hold people accountable. Instead you trust God to judge, to decide what punishment, if any, they must face.

Sometimes the one you forgive is dead and may not even know you forgave them. In that case, forgiveness is at least for *your* benefit.

Five young students including our son were killed because a young man got behind the wheel of a car while drunk. People died because of his choice. It would be easy to be angry at that young man and not forgive him. But not forgiving is sin which is harmful to us and those around us. Unforgiveness leads to bitterness, a place we do not want to go. We have chosen to forgive the driver completely with the help of the Holy Spirit. He may not be aware of our forgiveness since he died in The Accident, but we are. And more importantly, God is aware of our choice to forgive.

Let's look together at verses about forgiveness to learn what God says. Read the following and mark *forgive, hate,* and *love* in distinct ways. Note what these passages say about forgiveness.

Forgiveness

From these passages, is it okay to hate others?

Should we forgive *only* "brothers" who "ask"?

What happens if you do not forgive?

How does John describe those who love and those who hate?

How often should we forgive our brothers?

MATTHEW 6:14-15

[14] *For if you forgive others their trespasses, your heavenly Father will also forgive you,* [15] *but if you do not forgive others their trespasses, neither will your Father forgive your trespasses.*

MARK 11:25

[25] *And whenever you stand praying, forgive, if you have anything against anyone, so that your Father also who is in heaven may forgive you your trespasses.*

1 JOHN 2:9-11

[9] *Whoever says he is in the light and hates his brother is still in darkness.* [10] *Whoever loves his brother abides in the light, and in him there is no cause for stumbling.* [11] *But whoever hates his brother is in the darkness and walks in the darkness, and does not know where he is going, because the darkness has blinded his eyes.*

MATTHEW 18:21-22

[21] *Then Peter came up and said to him, "Lord, how often will my brother sin against me, and I forgive him? As many as seven times?"* [22] *Jesus said to him, "I do not say to you seven times, but seventy times seven.*

What "are" people who love their enemies?

How does "so that you may *be*" differ from "so that you may *become*"?

MATTHEW 5:43-46

[43] *"You have heard that it was said, 'You shall love your neighbor and hate your enemy.' [44] But I say to you, Love your enemies and pray for those who persecute you, [45] so that you may be sons of your Father who is in heaven. For he makes his sun rise on the evil and on the good, and sends rain on the just and on the unjust. [46] For if you love those who love you, what reward do you have? Do not even the tax collectors do the same?*

Summarize what you learned about forgiveness. Then ask God to show you anyone you need to forgive. Write a prayer asking Him to help you forgive even people responsible for the death of your loved one.

Just Journaling

Do you need to forgive someone you believe is responsible for your loved one's death? Are you willing to do it now? Ask the Holy Spirit to help you. Write about it or draw a picture in your Journal.

Is it Okay to be Angry?

When someone causes the death of someone you love, it's natural to be angry towards them. They may need to be held legally accountable. How should we act in our anger? Is it okay to hold on to our anger?

Earlier we asked, "What do we do with our feelings of anger, rage, and desire for revenge?" You looked at verses that teach us to put off anger, rage, and malice in previous lessons. Now let's look at a few verses about how we can control our anger.

Read the following and mark *anger* and any synonyms. Write what you learn about anger and how we are to behave. As you study these, think about how you can apply them to your anger towards the one responsible for your loved one's death.

NOTE: Some of these we've done already but they're important to review.

Anger

How To Behave

ECCLESIASTES 7:8-9

⁸ *Better is the end of a thing than its beginning, and the patient in spirit is better than the proud in spirit.* ⁹ *Be not quick in your spirit to become angry, for anger lodges in the heart of fools.*

Should we consider any bad event to be an end in itself—"The End!"?

What better perspective will help us be patient?

What's superior to physical strength?

Who decides what we might attribute to chance?

Are any occurrences "random" or do all events have reasons, purposes attached to them?

Whose purposes?

Is it possible to be angry and not sin?

Who do we help if we don't do this?

What time of day *should* our anger cease?

PROVERBS 16:32-33

32 Whoever is slow to anger is better than the mighty, and he who rules his spirit than he who takes a city. 33 The lot is cast into the lap, but its every decision is from the LORD.

ECCLESIASTES 3:1

3 For everything there is a season, and a time for every matter under heaven:

ISAIAH 46:10

*10 declaring the end from the beginning
and from ancient times things
not yet done,
saying, 'My counsel shall stand,
and I will accomplish all my
purpose,'*

EPHESIANS 1:11

11 In him we have obtained an inheritance, having been predestined according to the purpose of him who works all things according to the counsel of his will,

EPHESIANS 4:26-27.

26 Be angry and do not sin; do not let the sun go down on your anger, 27 and give no opportunity to the devil.

Anger

COLOSSIANS 3:5-10.

⁵ Put to death therefore what is earthly in you: sexual immorality, impurity, passion, evil desire, and covetousness, which is idolatry. ⁶ On account of these the wrath of God is coming. ⁷ In these you too once walked, when you were living in them. ⁸ But now you must put them all away: anger, wrath, malice, slander, and obscene talk from your mouth. ⁹ Do not lie to one another, seeing that you have put off the old self with its practices ¹⁰ and have put on the new self, which is being renewed in knowledge after the image of its creator.

How To Behave

JAMES 1:19-21

¹⁹ Know this, my beloved brothers: let every person be quick to hear, slow to speak, slow to anger; ²⁰ for the anger of man does not produce the righteousness of God. ²¹ Therefore put away all filthiness and rampant wickedness and receive with meekness the implanted word, which is able to save your souls.

Anger

How To Behave

EPHESIANS 4:31-32

³¹ Let all bitterness and wrath and anger and clamor and slander be put away from you, along with all malice. ³² Be kind to one another, tenderhearted, forgiving one another, as God in Christ forgave you.

Summarize what you learned about forgiveness and anger in this lesson including how you're responding to it.

Forgiving People Who Take Their Own Lives

One final point about forgiveness: If the person you are grieving committed suicide, you still need to forgive. You may be angry at him or her for leaving you or leaving other family behind but you must forgive . . . for your sake and out of obedience to God.

It hurts to lose someone we love to suicide; we've had both friends and one family member take their lives. Some were depressed; some were stuck in addictions they could not overcome; some couldn't stand the lives they were living. For whatever reason they did not think they had options. They preferred death to the life they saw ahead of them. Each time we learned a friend or family member died by suicide we were hurt, angry, upset, and sad. We felt so many emotions. The death of someone we care about tears us up inside as it is; death *by their own hand* makes it worse.

We can't undo what has been said and done. We can and must ask forgiveness when we sin. We can and must forgive others who have sinned against us or hurt us including those who have caused deaths, even their own. That is how we should respond as believers in Christ Jesus.

Do you need to forgive someone? Is there someone at fault for your loss? Did your loved one die by suicide? My dear friends we understand, and more importantly so does God. Pray. Talk to Him. Tell Him about your pain. Ask Him to help you forgive those who were at fault. Tell Him you are willing to forgive.

Just Journaling

Are you angry with someone? Do you blame someone for the death you are grieving? Write about your feelings and thoughts. Did someone you love take his or her own life? Write about what you learned in this lesson. Then write how you are going to respond to what you learned. Pray and ask God to help you forgive.

LESSON 14

How Can I Trust God Now?

Whoever loves father or mother more than me is not worthy of me, and whoever loves son or daughter more than me is not worthy of me. And whoever does not take his cross and follow me is not worthy of me. Whoever finds his life will lose it, and whoever loses his life for my sake will find it (Matthew 10:37-39).

Do you love Jesus more than anyone? Do you love Him more than those who have died? Dear One, do you love Him enough to trust Him?

Yes, we are wounded from our loss, but this is when we need His healing most. Jesus came to bind up the broken-hearted. When we are wounded, we need Jesus and His comfort; we need to trust Him as we grieve in order to heal.

Matthew 10:37-39 tells us that if we do not take up our cross and follow Jesus we are not worthy of Him. Are you willing to follow Jesus even when you do not understand? Are you willing to be transformed into His image during your grief? Are you willing to take a step towards trusting Him as He heals you and uses your suffering for His glory and your good? To be transformed by God into the image of Christ and to find healing in our grief, we must trust Him.

You may be thinking, "But how can I trust God when He did not save my loved one's life?" Beloved, even without answers to why things happen the way they do, we can trust God because of His nature. We have seen that He is compassionate, gracious, loving, full of mercy, and just. He is a good and loving Father. He is the Creator of the Universe. He is God and is worthy of our worship. He is faithful and His promises are true.

People who have lost someone they love often say things like "I don't trust God anymore" or "I can't pray since He didn't answer my prayer for my mom to be healed" or "I'm too angry with God to pray or go to church." If you have said these things or felt this way, working through this lesson will help you find truth to change the way you're thinking. If you need to, go back and read the lessons on *Comfort in Grief* and *Do You Still Believe?* They are full of truth about the nature of God. If we know His nature, we know what to trust and why.

God is God, we are not; God controls life and death, we don't. This is hard to reconcile with our preconceived ideas of how things should work, but we're not required to "figure it all out." We *are* required to respond obediently to bad circumstances and learn from His Word. Are you willing to be transformed by God? As you work through this lesson, listen to the Holy Spirit teaching you truth, then ask God to help you apply what you learned to your life.

Anger at God

One platitude some have said to us supposedly to help us in our grief is this: "It's okay to be angry with God. He is big enough to handle it."

Some well-intentioned (or so they think) people will even tell you that if you don't admit you're angry with God you're "in denial." Accordingly, a friend of ours asked us if we were "angry with God *yet*." When we told her we had never been angry with God over the things that had happened in the past year, she said with an angry sneer, *"You will be!* You better do it soon; if you don't you'll never be truly healthy!" We quickly realized that she was not someone from whom we should seek counsel.

Yes, God is big enough to handle our anger. But is it okay to be angry at Him? Does the fact that we're created in His image justify our adversely judging Him?

What is the basis of anger? When you're angry with someone, aren't you saying he has wronged you in some way? Then isn't anger with God saying that the Creator of the Universe "wronged" you? Doesn't this put you in the place of judge? When you express anger at God, you attack His character; you're saying, "You wronged me! You can't be trusted! I could do this whole 'rule the world thing' better than You!"

Yes, He wants us to honestly cry out to Him in our grief. He wants us to tell Him our thoughts and lean on Him for comfort. But it's arrogant to think we have a right to be angry with God. He is the Creator of all things!

In an earlier lesson we looked at how God responded to Job when he questioned Him. Read Job 40:6-14 and mark *the Lord* and all pronouns that refer to Him. List what you learn about God in this passage.

God	**JOB 40:6-14**

How did God respond to Job when he questioned Him?	⁶ *Then the LORD answered Job out of the whirlwind and said:*
	 ⁷ *"Dress for action like a man;*
	   I will question you, and you
	      make it known to me.
	 ⁸ *Will you even put me in the*
	      wrong?
	   Will you condemn me that you
	      may be in the right?
	 ⁹ *Have you an arm like God,*
	   and can you thunder with a
	      voice like his?"

What does He tell him to do?	¹⁰ *"Adorn yourself with majesty*
	   and dignity; clothe yourself
	      with glory and splendor.
	 ¹¹ *Pour out the overflowings of*
	      your anger,
	   and look on everyone who is
	      proud and abase him.
	 ¹² *Look on everyone who is proud*
	      and bring him low
	   and tread down the wicked
	      where they stand.
	 ¹³ *Hide them all in the dust*
	      together;
	   bind their faces in the world
	      below.

Why?—What does the "then" in v. 14 imply?	¹⁴ *Then will I also acknowledge to*
	      you
	   that your own right hand can
	      save you.

Read Job 42:1-6. Mark *Job* and all pronouns that refer to him.

What does Job concede in verses 2–4?

JOB 42:1-6

[1] *Then Job answered the L<small>ORD</small> and said:*
2   *"I know that you can do all things,*
          and that no purpose of yours can
          be thwarted.
3   *'Who is this that hides counsel*
          without knowledge?'
      Therefore I have uttered what I did
          not understand,
          things too wonderful for me, which
          I did not know.
4   *'Hear, and I will speak;*
          I will question you, and you make
          it known to me.'
5   *I had heard of you by the hearing of*
          the ear,
          but now my eye sees you;
6   *therefore I despise myself,*
          and repent in dust and ashes."

How does he respond to God in verses 5-6?

God welcomes our honest questions. He wants us to humbly come to Him with our concerns and doubts. But it's sin to stand in judgment over Him, to believe He's below us and answers to us, to call His truth into account as if *we* were *His* God.

Consider this: "all the inhabitants of the earth are accounted *as nothing,* and He does according to his will among the host of heaven and among the inhabitants of the earth; and none can stay his hand or say to him, *"What have you done?"* (Daniel 4:35). We can question God as Jesus did on the cross ("Why have you forsaken me?") but we shouldn't criticize Him ("You did the wrong thing!"). We can't do that without His calling us into account for it. He doesn't want us to think bad thoughts about Him because . . . He's not bad. We just don't have the full picture yet, but we will one day.

How do we deal with anger towards God? Like every sin: confess it and ask His forgiveness! He will forgive those who sincerely repent. Then get into the Word to remind yourself of His good, loving sovereignty.

Read the following verses and mark all references to *God* and *Jesus* and their synonyms. List what you learn about God. Add these to your list of what you learned about God.

God

1 TIMOTHY 6:13-16

[13] I charge you in the presence of God, who gives life to all things, and of Christ Jesus, who in his testimony before Pontius Pilate made the good confession, [14] to keep the commandment unstained and free from reproach until the appearing of our Lord Jesus Christ, [15] which he will display at the proper time—he who is the blessed and only Sovereign, the King of kings and Lord of lords, [16] who alone has immortality, who dwells in unapproachable light, whom no one has ever seen or can see. To him be honor and eternal dominion. Amen.

DEUTERONOMY 10:17-18

[17] For the Lord your God is God of gods and Lord of lords, the great, the mighty, and the awesome God, who is not partial and takes no bribe. [18] He executes justice for the fatherless and the widow, and loves the sojourner, giving him food and clothing.

1 CHRONICLES 29:10-12

[10] Therefore David blessed the Lord in the presence of all the assembly. And David said: "Blessed are you, O Lord, the God of Israel our father, forever and ever. [11] Yours, O Lord, is the greatness and the power and the glory and the victory and the majesty, for all that is in the heavens and in the earth is yours. Yours is the kingdom, O Lord, and you

God

Note the key repeated phrase "for his steadfast love endures forever" in Psalm 136. What two attributes does this Psalm link together?

Continue to list what you learn about God.

are exalted as head above all. *¹² Both riches and honor come from you, and you rule over all. In your hand are power and might, and in your hand it is to make great and to give strength to all.*

PSALM 136:1-9

*¹ Give thanks to the L*ORD*, for he is good,*
    for his steadfast love endures forever.
² Give thanks to the God of gods,
    for his steadfast love endures forever.
³ Give thanks to the Lord of lords,
    for his steadfast love endures forever;
⁴ to him who alone does great wonders,
    for his steadfast love endures forever;
⁵ to him who by understanding made the heavens,
    for his steadfast love endures forever;
⁶ to him who spread out the earth above the waters,
    for his steadfast love endures forever;
⁷ to him who made the great lights,
    for his steadfast love endures forever;
⁸ the sun to rule over the day,
    for his steadfast love endures forever;
⁹ the moon and stars to rule over the night,
    for his steadfast love endures forever.

God

PSALM 46:8-11

[8] *Come, behold the works of the LORD,*
how he has brought desolations
on the earth.
[9] *He makes wars cease to the end of the*
earth;
he breaks the bow and shatters
the spear;
he burns the chariots with fire.
[10] *"Be still, and know that I am God.*
I will be exalted among the
nations,
I will be exalted in the earth!"
[11] *The LORD of hosts is with us;*
the God of Jacob is our fortress.
Selah

List the attributes God alone has.

PSALM 103:19

[19] *The LORD has established his throne in*
the heavens,
and his kingdom rules over all.

List classes of people God particularly helps.

List all the things the Lord rules over.

Write what you are thinking about what you learned.

In a later lesson we will study Psalm 103 and Psalm 23. Both teach us about the nature of God and what He does for us. King David often cried out to God in his distress. He knew the Lord. Even in his darkest times—his sons' deaths, enemies surrounding, Nathan's confrontation—David cried out to God, seeking the counsel and help only He can give. He praised God in the good times and in the dark times. You will find reading the Psalms especially helpful as you seek truth about God, reminding yourself that He indeed is the Loving King of kings and Lord of lords. Though we're His bond-servants, He calls us sons.

Beloved, can you clothe yourself in majesty, glory and splendor as the Lord does? Were you there when the foundations of the world were laid? If we don't have the knowledge to criticize God, can we possibly have the right to attack His sovereignty? Isn't His sovereignty both wise and good even if we can't see that now? Isn't God over all of this and isn't He compassionate and good and kind by nature? Wasn't it the kindness of God that led you to repentance? He gave you your loved one in the first place; do you think He'll abandon you now? Do you think He has abandoned your loved one? Death can't separate us from the love of God which is in Christ Jesus our Lord (Romans 8:38-39).

These are better questions to ask and the right judgments about God that answer them come right from His Word. But If you've been criticizing Him, confess it quickly and talk to Him about it. He loves you and wants to comfort you. He wants to have a close relationship with you. He wants to restore you . . . now!

Just Journaling

Summarize what you learned about anger towards God. Then, take time to write out your thoughts and feelings about what you have read. If you need

to, confess your anger to God and tell Him you've been wrong to judge Him.
Write out your prayer of confession. Tell Him what you believe about Him.
We have more space in our Journal for you to write.

Learning to Pray After Loss

When we lost our parents and our son on separate occasions we immediately turned to God. We cried out to Him in our pain. We had both been Christians and studied the Word for years and knew the Lord's nature. We knew He loved us and though we did not understand everything we knew we could trust Him.

This is not the case for everyone. The death of a loved one shakes faith to its very core and can cause you to question how to pray.

Many of us have prayed for healing or protection for our family members but they died anyway. It doesn't appear that God answered our prayers. Is that appearance correct? Does the death of a loved one mean God did not answer our prayer?

If you're struggling at all with prayer, first go back to the early lessons of this study (or to your list of "What I Learned About God") and review God's nature. Review what you learned about your position in Christ in Lesson 11. When we know God's nature and our position in Christ, it becomes easier to pray. Prayer is talking to a good friend we know loves us. Knowing that our Heavenly Father is compassionate, gracious, slow to anger, and full of love makes it easier to talk to Him.

Does God answer our prayers? Read the following passages and underline *call,* *cries out,* and other references to *prayer*. Note what you learn about conditions to approaching God and promises made.

According to these passages do we get everything we ask for? Note how we're to approach God and what He promises.

Approaching God

Promises Made

PSALM 91:14-15

14 *"Because he holds fast to me in love, I will deliver him;*
I will protect him, because he knows my name.
15 *When he calls to me, I will answer him;*
I will be with him in trouble;
I will rescue him and honor him.

ISAIAH 58:9-11

9 *Then you shall call, and the* Lord *will answer;*
you shall cry, and he will say, 'Here I am.'
If you take away the yoke from our midst,
the pointing of the finger, and speaking wickedness,
10 *if you pour yourself out for the hungry*
and satisfy the desire of the afflicted,
then shall your light rise in the darkness
and your gloom be as the noonday.
11 *And the* Lord *will guide you continually*
and satisfy your desire in scorched places
and make your bones strong;
and you shall be like a watered garden,
like a spring of water,
whose waters do not fail.

Approaching God

LUKE 11:10-13

[10] For everyone who asks receives, and the one who seeks finds, and to the one who knocks it will be opened. [11] What father among you, if his son asks for a fish, will instead of a fish give him a serpent; [12] or if he asks for an egg, will give him a scorpion? [13] If you then, who are evil, know how to give good gifts to your children, how much more will the heavenly Father give the Holy Spirit to those who ask him!"

Promises Made

JAMES 1:5-8

[5] If any of you lacks wisdom, let him ask God, who gives generously to all without reproach, and it will be given him. [6] But let him ask in faith, with no doubting, for the one who doubts is like a wave of the sea that is driven and tossed by the wind. [7] For that person must not suppose that he will receive anything from the Lord; [8] he is a double-minded man, unstable in all his ways.

Context matters to Bible study! Many struggle with trusting God because they have misconceptions of what the Bible teaches; they have heard wrong teaching. Contexts help us correct misinterpretations of single verses. When we study scriptures in their contexts and apply their truths to our lives, we find healing, hope, peace, and joy.

Continue reading the following passages and underline *call, cries out*, and other references to *prayer*. Note again what you learn about conditions God advises in our approach to Him and promises He makes.

Approaching God

JOHN 15:5-8

[5] *I am the vine; you are the branches. Whoever abides in me and I in him, he it is that bears much fruit, for apart from me you can do nothing.* [6] *If anyone does not abide in me he is thrown away like a branch and withers; and the branches are gathered, thrown into the fire, and burned.* [7] *If you abide in me, and my words abide in you, ask whatever you wish, and it will be done for you.* [8] *By this my Father is glorified, that you bear much fruit and so prove to be my disciples.*

Promises Made

1 JOHN 3:21-22

[21] *Beloved, if our heart does not condemn us, we have confidence before God;* [22] *and whatever we ask we receive from him, because we keep his commandments and do what pleases him.*

Unfortunately, there have always been some in the Church right up to today who teach that it's God's will to give us everything we ask for. Beloved, that's not how God works; that's not how prayer works; we don't get to order God to do things like a waiter or butler. He's not our servant.

We can know God is sovereign, but John clearly tells us "And this is the confidence that we have toward him, that if we ask anything *according to His will* He hears us" (1 John 5:14). It's up to us to find out from His Word what His will is. We know He wants a relationship with us and prayer is a vital part of that relationship. Prayer is speaking to God but we first have to listen to His Word to learn His will, what He wants us to speak to Him about.

Read the following passages and mark *pray, prayer,* and *supplication*. Note what you learn about prayer.

Prayer

PHILIPPIANS 4:4-7

[4] *Rejoice in the Lord always; again I will say, rejoice.* [5] *Let your reasonableness be known to everyone. The Lord is at hand;* [6] *do not be anxious about anything, but in everything by prayer and supplication with thanksgiving let your requests be made known to God.* [7] *And the peace of God, which surpasses all understanding, will guard your hearts and your minds in Christ Jesus.*

1 THESSALONIANS 5:16-18

[16] *Rejoice always,* [17] *pray without ceasing,* [18] *give thanks in all circumstances; for this is the will of God in Christ Jesus for you.*

EPHESIANS 6:16-18

[16] *In all circumstances take up the shield of faith, with which you can extinguish all the flaming darts of the evil one;* [17] *and take the helmet of salvation, and the sword of the Spirit, which is the word of God,* [18] *praying at all times in the Spirit, with all prayer and supplication. To that end, keep alert with all perseverance, making supplication for all the saints.*

We're called to pray, to ask God for things, holy things. Because He's a loving Father we can take all our anxieties to Him and He will calm us one way or the other according to His will. Beloved, as we studied in an earlier lesson God cares for you *and* knows what's best. He is, after all, God! Will you trust Him, step by step, day by day, little by little? Will you take the step of simply crying out to Him in your grief today? Tell Him how you're feeling. Tell Him what you're thinking. He knows you and loves you. Trust Him. He is worthy of your trust.

Just Journaling

In your Journal, list what you have learned about prayer. Copy verses that stood out to you. Then write a prayer asking God to help you trust Him. Ask Him to help you pray and to hear His voice.

Praying Scripture

*[**Kathleen**] One reason I can pray and trust God to answer early in my grief is that many years ago I realized that I did not know how to pray, so I decided to find out. I studied the Bible to learn what God says about prayer and applied what I learned. I realized I had been giving Him a "wish-list" of things I wanted Him to do for me without any regard to what He wanted. I was giving God my wish list without listening to Him.*

By studying Scripture and applying it in my life I learned to use the written Word of God to pray according to God's will for my family and friends. This replaced the list that was not only selfish but foolish—namely the thought that I could conceive an "answer" better than He could. It was hardly a novel idea; using scriptures to compose prayers is a very ancient concept and practice. But it was new for me and it transformed my prayer life.

When my mom died I prayed using Scripture and found comfort in the passages I had learned. Sixteen years later when our son died, I had memorized many of Jesus and Paul's prayers along with other passages of Scripture. I cried out in my sorrow to the God I knew using His Word.

Often when we're hurting we don't know how to pray; we're distracted by so many bad thoughts. Learning to pray using Scripture is a good place to start. When we pray Scripture we're using words our Creator-Redeemer inspired. Praying the words Jesus taught His disciples to pray and the prayers of the writers of the New Testament help us pray even when we're weighed down by grief. They can pick you up and out of a very deep pit.

You may want to write out your prayers instead of speaking them. You may have noticed that many of your *Just Journaling* prompts ask you to write out your prayers. This is intentional. We want you to learn to trust God and pray as you wander unwillingly down Grief Road looking for relief, patiently waiting for the Lord's permanent exit when He returns for you. As we have learned, time spent doing the right things—seeking the Lord, studying and applying His Word, and doing the next right thing—will help you find healing, hope, peace and joy. Prayer is one big part of this healing journey. You may want to go back through earlier lessons and read the prayers you wrote. See how God has answered your prayers and how He is helping you heal in your grief,

We know from the Bible that we're to pray for ourselves and each other. The Word consistently commands believers to pray; it doesn't suggest, advise, hint at. Throughout the Old and New Testaments we see godly men and women presenting their requests to God, waiting for Him, and eventually seeing His awesome responses. God does not always answer the way we want Him to answer but His answers are wisest and best. As a loving Father, He hears and answers the prayers of His children.

If you're finding it difficult to pray, start with simple prayers. Cry out to God and honestly tell Him what you're feeling. Pray what Jesus taught; "the Lord's Prayer" may seem simple on the surface but it's powerful underneath. It covers God's glory and our needs. We know some bereaved parents who said this prayer was "the only one [they] could manage for a long time." Praying it daily helped them keep their focus on God during oppressive sorrow and helped them learned to pray again.

Read Matthew 6:9-13 and note what you learn about God.

God	**MATTHEW 6:9-13**
	⁹ Pray then like this:
	"Our Father in heaven,
	hallowed be your name.
	¹⁰ Your kingdom come,
	your will be done,
	on earth as it is in heaven.
	¹¹ Give us this day our daily bread,
	¹² and forgive us our debts,
	as we also have forgiven our debtors.
	¹³ And lead us not into temptation,
	but deliver us from evil.

Look closely at each verse. How do they line up with what you've learned in this study about God's provision for you and your attitude towards others?

Try praying this prayer for yourself. Maybe write it out in your *Journal*.

Will you commit to praying it each day for a week? We believe that taking this small step will help you heal.

Praying Paul's Prayers and the Psalms

Praying the prayers of Paul can be helpful when learning to pray. Here's an example of a prayer Kathleen wrote for our son a few years before he died using Paul's prayer from Ephesians 1:15-20:

> *Father,*
>
> *Andrew knows You. He knows Your truth and He knows Your Son, but he's making unwise choices right now. Please give him the Spirit of wisdom and revelation so that he will know You better. I ask You to open the eyes of Andrew's heart so that he will know the hope to which You have called him. And help him to act on that hope. I pray that he will understand the riches of the inheritance available to him as a saint and that Andrew will know Your incomparably great power for him, a believer. Help him remember that Christ was raised from the dead and sits at Your right hand. I know Your power that raised Christ from the dead is available to Andrew. Help him know that this power is for him today as he faces battles in life.*
>
> *Amen.*

Our son did know the hope to which he had been called. He came to understand the riches of God's glorious inheritance. He is living that glorious inheritance now in the presence of Christ. God answered this prayer, obviously not the way we preferred, but He did answer.

Now let's look at what Paul prayed for believers. His prayers are appropriate for us today as well. Mark anything that stands out to you in these passages and note what you learn. Look carefully at each one. Note what the focus of each prayer is. Are these things you want in your life and in the lives of your family and friends? Make a list of things from these passages you can pray for yourself and others.

Prayer Focus

EPHESIANS 1:15-20

[15] *For this reason, because I have heard of your faith in the Lord Jesus and your love[j] toward all the saints,* [16] *I do not cease to give thanks for you, remembering you in my prayers,* [17] *that the God of our Lord Jesus Christ, the Father of glory, may give you the Spirit of wisdom and of revelation in the knowledge of him,* [18] *having the eyes of your hearts enlightened, that you may know what is the hope to which he has called you, what are the riches of his glorious inheritance in the saints,* [19] *and what is the immeasurable greatness of his power toward us who believe, according to the working of his great might* [20] *that he worked in Christ when he raised him from the dead and seated him at his right hand in the heavenly places.*

PHILIPPIANS 1:9-11

[9] *And it is my prayer that your love may abound more and more, with knowledge and all discernment,* [10] *so that you may approve what is excellent, and so be pure and blameless for the day of Christ,* [11] *filled with the fruit of righteousness that comes through Jesus Christ, to the glory and praise of God.*

EPHESIANS 3:14-19

[14] *For this reason I bow my knees before the Father,* [15] *from whom every family in heaven and on earth is named,* [16] *that according to the riches of his glory he may grant you to be strengthened with power through his Spirit in your inner being,* [17] *so that Christ may dwell in*

Prayer Focus

your hearts through faith—that you, being rooted and grounded in love, [18] may have strength to comprehend with all the saints what is the breadth and length and height and depth, [19] and to know the love of Christ that surpasses knowledge, that you may be filled with all the fullness of God.

COLOSSIANS 1:9-14

[9] And so, from the day we heard, we have not ceased to pray for you, asking that you may be filled with the knowledge of his will in all spiritual wisdom and understanding, [10] so as to walk in a manner worthy of the Lord, fully pleasing to him, bearing fruit in every good work and increasing in the knowledge of God; [11] being strengthened with all power, according to his glorious might, for all endurance and patience with joy; [12] giving thanks to the Father, who has qualified you to share in the inheritance of the saints in light. [13] He has delivered us from the domain of darkness and transferred us to the kingdom of his beloved Son, [14] in whom we have redemption, the forgiveness of sins.

GALATIANS 1:3-5

[3] Grace to you and peace from God our Father and the Lord Jesus Christ, [4] who gave himself for our sins to deliver us from the present evil age, according to the will of our God and Father, [5] to whom be the glory forever and ever. Amen.

Did you notice the focus of these prayers—transformation into the image of Christ and growing closer to God by walking with Him? Using the list of what you learned in these passages, write out a prayer for yourself and someone you care about.

We have even used Paul's greetings in his epistles for prayers. For example, you can pray Galatians 1:3-5 for your friends. This prayer is simple. It's our prayer for you who are reading this today:

> *We pray grace to you and peace from God our Father and the Lord Jesus Christ, who gave himself for our sins to deliver us from the present evil age, according to the will of our God and Father, to whom be the glory forever and ever. Amen.*

Just Journaling

After you've marked these passages and noted their focus read each one aloud. Turn one or more of the ones you love into a prayer for a specific person. Write your prayer in your Journal.

The psalms are full of passages that easily convert to prayers. David cried out to God in his pain. He told God honestly about his struggles. He praised God in the middle of the storms of his life. In the first lesson of this book, you read a prayer using passages from Psalm 119. Now read Psalm 1 and write a prayer for people you care about ending with yourself. Use the promises in this psalm.

PSALM 1

> [1] *Blessed is the man who walks not in the counsel of the wicked, nor stands in the way of sinners, nor sits in the seat of scoffers;* [2] *but his delight is in the law of the LORD, and on his law he meditates day and night.* [3] *He is like a tree planted by streams of water that yields its fruit in its season, and its leaf does not wither. In all that he does, he prospers.* [4] *The wicked are not so, but are like chaff that the wind drives away.* [5] *Therefore the wicked will not stand in the judgment, nor sinners in the congregation of the righteous;* [6] *for the LORD knows the way of the righteous, but the way of the wicked will perish.*

When we suffer a loss it's hard to trust God and pray. Dear one, trusting God is our only choice! Life without Him is miserable and death more so. Life without Him leads to hell. Trusting him leads to peace and eternal life. When we know

His nature is loving Father, we can trust Him. When we know what He did for us, what He does for us, and what He promises for us, we can run to Him with our troubles and cry out to Him knowing He will love and care for us. He will comfort us. He will lead us in the way everlasting (Psalm 139:24).

When you don't know what to pray, praying Scripture is the best starting place. Find Jesus and Paul's prayers using an online concordance. Read through the Psalms and New Testament epistles and turn the words into *your* prayers. You'll be blessed!

Just Journaling

A few more of Paul's prayers are 1 Thessalonians 3:12-13, 2 Thessalonians 1:11-12, and Philippians 1:3-6. Using one of these, a favorite Psalm, or one of Paul's greetings, write out a prayer for yourself today. Then write a prayer for someone else.

Church

Trusting God and praying is difficult after a loss, but going to church may seem impossible! Many who grieve have told us they find it hard to walk back into the sanctuary where the funeral was held. Songs sung at the memorial hit us right in the gut. But we need fellowship with other Christians. We need to be a part of the body of believers. We need good Bible-based teaching. We need these things in order to heal. And the Body of Christ *needs us!*

Beloved, it is okay to step back from some of your responsibilities at church while you're mourning. We often don't have the energy to lead Bible studies or choir when we're dealing with deep grief. Grief is fatigue, among other things. Talk to your pastor or those in charge; let them know you need to take a break and that you'll advise when you're ready to step back in.

You may need to meet with your Sunday school or small-group leader in private to let him know what you need. Some of us are very sensitive and don't want to talk about our loss, even with our small group, for a while. Others of us want opportunities to share what happened. Meeting with your small group leader to discuss your needs and the needs of the group may help you ease back into participation.

But please, dear one, do not walk away from the Body! We need the love and compassion of the Body of Christ when we're hurting. No, they're not perfect and may say something unwise (to say the least), but they want to love you and help you heal. And they need you to help them learn about suffering and grief and the offsetting comfort and healing available in Christ. They know that they and others they know will face it sooner or later. God works through flawed, broken people. Will you let Him work through you?

Read Hebrews 10:19-25 and list the instructions along with any reasons given.

Instructions / Reasons	**HEBREWS 10:19-25**
	[19] Therefore, brothers, since we have confidence to enter the holy places by the blood of Jesus, [20] by the new and living way that he opened for us through the curtain, that is, through his flesh, [21] and since we have a great priest over the house of God, [22] let us draw near with a true heart in full assurance of faith, with our hearts sprinkled clean from an evil conscience and our bodies washed with pure water. [23] Let us hold fast the confession of our hope without wavering, for he who promised is faithful. [24] And let us consider how to stir up one another to love and good works, [25] not neglecting to meet together, as is the habit of some, but encouraging one another, and all the more as you see the Day drawing near.

Do you see the flow of this passage—from knowing what Christ did for us to being a part of His Body? When we understand all He has done and who we are in Christ, we'll want to be with like-minded believers.

Read Philippians 2:1-2. Yes, we've looked at this passage before but let's view it from another angle.

PHILIPPIANS 2:1-2

> *¹ So if there is any encouragement in Christ, any comfort from love, any participation in the Spirit, any affection and sympathy, ² complete my joy by being of the same mind, having the same love, being in full accord and of one mind.*

Yes, going to church after loss is an emotional event; it's difficult. You'll be uncomfortable and people you meet will be uncomfortable . . . initially. But it's one way to move forward in your grief.

Have you received encouragement, comfort, and affection from Christ in your grief journey?

If so, how can you use this to help others who are deeply hurting? List what God tells us.

Can you do these things if you isolate yourself from the rest of the Body of Christ?

We know going back to church after a loss is difficult, but it's vital to remain part of the body of believers. Many people we know who have lost loved ones tell us that certain songs in church trigger grief. They often cry during the song part of worship. That's okay! Tears are not sin and neither is sadness. In fact, as God tracks our Grief wanderings He puts our tears in two places because they're precious to Him: His bottle and His book (Psalm 56:8). When "the books [are] opened" on that Day (Daniel 7:10, Revelation 20:12), that's where they'll be. In addition to the precious tears that so value your love for your lost loved one, it will be good to have godly sorrow for sin recorded on the Asset side of the balance sheet.

Going to church with someone will help you step back into your church and small group. Having an understanding friend alongside will make you more comfortable walking back in.

> *[Kathleen] A sweet couple sit next to us each Sunday. Mary has taken on herself to make sure there's always a box of tissues nearby since she knows my tears will flow at any mention of Heaven, redemption, or the*

crucifixion. Knowing they will be there each week with a smile and a hug helps me go to church on my more tender, vulnerable days. It's not that I'm sad or upset while singing; rather, these things are more real to me now! I'm grateful that our parents and our son knew Jesus as their Savior and are now alive with Him in Heaven. When we sing about such things, I sing joyfully even as my tears run down my face.

Beloved, if you have experienced loss and have walked away from church in your grief, please consider going back. If you left because you decided the church you attended was not for you, then find another Bible-believing church. We have heard from many who said their church family was a life-line during their mourning. Others have changed churches for various reasons. Please dear one, talk with your family, pray and seek God, then find a God-trusting, Bible-teaching place to worship and gather with its believers to worship, praise, pray, sing, and hear God's truths.

You need them and they need you.

Just Journaling

If your church family has been helpful to you in your grief, write about it. Some of us find it hard to write lots of thank-you notes after losing someone we love. Write one thank-you note to your church family expressing how much they mean to you. Perhaps you can list specific things people did to help you. You may want to copy your note in your Journal and then mail it to your pastor. He will be encouraged by seeing how you were helped.

If your church did not help you, or if you are not part of a local body of believers, write a prayer asking God to direct you in finding a local body where you can be a part. List friends who you know attend church regularly. Then call one of them to ask if you could go to church with them this week.

LESSON 15

Do We Become Angels When We Die?

[Kathleen} My mother-in-law was one of the sweetest and kindest women I have ever met. Rita helped me learn to be a good mom. I was honored to help care for her in the last weeks of her life as she lay dying from pancreatic cancer. In the nearly thirty years I knew her I do not recall her ever saying anything bad about anyone. She was a doll. No, she was not literally a doll; I use that word as a term of endearment.

Our son was killed along with four friends coming home from an end-of-the-season cookout. They were all part of the outdoor musical "Texas." Many of their friends refer to them now as the "Texas Angels." This too is a term of endearment, not a theological statement. It's simply a phrase to describe their character. These five young people were certainly talented but they were also kind, compassionate, and caring towards their families and their fellow cast mates. They were "angels" in this sense.

But in what sense if any did they become angels when they died? For example, are they, as some think, "guardians"? Do they watch over us?

What does the Bible say about angels and people after death? Do people become angels when they die? Do they "gain their wings" as many say?

Read the following passages. Underline *angels* and draw a box around *man* and any synonyms. Note what you learn.

NOTE
The Old Testament was written in Hebrew with a splash of Aramaic. The Hebrew word for "angel" is malak which means "messenger," "representative."
The New Testament was written in Greek, with a very few Aramaic words. The Greek word translated "angel" is aggelos which means "messenger," "envoy," "one sent."

What "image" was man made in?

GENESIS 1:26-27

26 Then God said, "Let us make man in our image, after our likeness. And let them have dominion over the fish of the sea and over the birds of the heavens and over the livestock and over all the earth and over every creeping thing that creeps on the earth." 27 So God created man in his own image, in the image of God he created him; male and female he created them.

Who will judge angels?

1 CORINTHIANS 6:3

3 Do you not know that we are to judge angels? How much more, then, matters pertaining to this life!

What does this tell you about the relative rank of man in the coming age?

What does Jesus say in verse 36?

LUKE 20:34-38

34 And Jesus said to them, "The sons of this age marry and are given in marriage, 35 but those who are considered worthy to attain to that age and to the resurrection from the dead neither marry nor are given in marriage, 36 for they cannot die anymore, because they are equal to angels and are sons of God, being sons of the resurrection. 37 But that the dead are raised, even Moses showed, in the passage about the bush, where he calls the Lord the God of Abraham and the God of Isaac and the God of Jacob. 38 Now he is not God of the dead, but of the living, for all live to him."

Does "equal to angels" mean "angels" or are resurrected people still distinct?

Who does Moses call the Lord "the God of"?

While Moses wrote this, who actually said it? (See Exodus 3:6.)

What do the tenses of "is," "living," and "live" in verse 38 tell you about those who have died?

Do these teachings bring you comfort regarding your loved one? What are you thinking after studying them?

Hebrews 12:22-24 is addressed to believers. The writer tells them they have come to the city of the living God. Notice who else is in the city. List the groups that are dwelling in the city.

Groups in City	**HEBREWS 12:22-24**
	²² But you have come to Mount Zion and to the city of the living God, the heavenly Jerusalem, and to innumerable angels in festal gathering, ²³ and to the assembly of the firstborn who are enrolled in heaven, and to God, the judge of all, and to the spirits of the righteous made perfect, ²⁴ and to Jesus, the mediator of a new covenant, and to the sprinkled blood that speaks a better word than the blood of Abel.

Are the "innumerable angels" and the "spirits of the righteous made perfect" the same creatures? What key word makes them the same or different?

Whom do angels serve?

Who are "those who are to inherit salvation"?

Are the angels "sent out to serve" and "those who are to inherit salvation" the same beings? What key words tell us one way or the other?

HEBREWS 1:13-14

13 And to which of the angels has he ever said, "Sit at my right hand until I make your enemies a footstool for your feet"? 14 Are they not all ministering spirits sent out to serve for the sake of those who are to inherit salvation?

Who does God help and who does He not help?

HEBREWS 2:16

16 For surely it is not angels that he helps, but he helps the offspring of Abraham.

The Old Testament contains stories of angels disguised as men that God sent to do things. Those to whom the angels were sent did not at first recognize them as angels. From this we learn that angels may have the external form (shape) of humans, but they remain angels.

Just Journaling

Did you think people become angels when they die? Do you believe this after studying these passages? Write what you know to be true about angels. Make a list of what you have learned about angels in your Journal.

Some people find that describing their lost loved ones with words like "dead," "death," or "died" is too painful to bear. Instead they substitute phrases like "earned his wings" or "became an angel." Some refer to their loved ones as "our angel." Others use the term "angel" as a term of endearment. But Scripture teaches that humans were created in God's image. We are different and separate from angels. We don't become angels when we die.

Some believe that our loved ones become angels to watch over and guard us when they die. Did you believe this before this study? What do you believe now?

Let's hone our study to focus on the guardian part.

Guardian Angels

Though *we* do not become angels when we die, Scripture does teach that some angels watch over us and protect us.

Read these passages and note what you learn about angels.

Angels	PSALM 103:20-21
To whom do the angels answer?	*²⁰ Bless the LORD, O you his angels, you mighty ones who do his word, obeying the voice of his word! ²¹ Bless the LORD, all his hosts, his ministers, who do his will!*

Search the Old Testament term "hosts" in an online concordance (or hard copy) to see if you can determine what the hosts of the Lord are. Write out some key verses:

Angels

What does "the angel of the LORD" do for those who fear the LORD?

Who are we to take refuge in?

Psalm 91:1-2, 11. What terms tell us we're secure in the LORD?

Who is our refuge?

Who commands the angels? What are they commanded to do?

What did God send to help Daniel?

Why?

PSALM 34:4-8

4 I sought the LORD, and he answered me and delivered me from all my fears. 5 Those who look to him are radiant, and their faces shall never be ashamed. 6 This poor man cried, and the LORD heard him and saved him out of all his troubles. 7 The angel of the LORD encamps around those who fear him, and delivers them. 8 Oh, taste and see that the LORD is good! Blessed is the man who takes refuge in him!

PSALM 91:1-2, 11

1 He who dwells in the shelter of the Most High will abide in the shadow of the Almighty. 2 I will say to the LORD, "My refuge and my fortress, my God, in whom I trust

11 For he will command his angels concerning you to guard you in all your ways."

DANIEL 6:21-22

21 Then Daniel said to the king, "O king, live forever! 22 My God sent his angel and shut the lions' mouths, and they have not harmed me, because I was found blameless before him; and also before you, O king, I have done no harm."

Scripture forbids worshipping and serving angels (Deuteronomy 4:19) which are simply higher-order creatures (Nehemiah 9:6; Psalm 33:6; Isaiah 45:12). We're not to put our faith in them. God created them and God is sovereign over them. If we need help, we go to the Commander of the hosts. He decides who to send and what to do.

Read the following verses. Mark key words that tell us how to relate to the Lord and note what you learn. Note especially terms that describe contrasts and uniqueness.

Key Words: Relating to the Lord

PROVERBS 3:5-8

5 Trust in the LORD with all your heart, and do not lean on your own understanding. 6 In all your ways acknowledge him, and he will make straight your paths. 7 Be not wise in your own eyes; fear the LORD, and turn away from evil. 8 It will be healing to your flesh and refreshment to your bones.

PSALM 62:1-2, 8

1 For God alone my soul waits in silence; from him comes my salvation. 2 He alone is my rock and my salvation, my fortress; I shall not be greatly shaken.

8 Trust in him at all times, O people; pour out your heart before him; God is a refuge for us.

PSALM 20:7-8

7 Some trust in chariots and some in horses, but we trust in the name of the LORD our God. 8 They collapse and fall, but we rise and stand upright.

Finally, look at Hebrews 12:1-2. Note what you learn about Jesus in this passage.

Jesus	HEBREWS 12:1-2
	¹ Therefore, since we are surrounded by so great a cloud of witnesses, let us also lay aside every weight, and sin which clings so closely, and let us run with endurance the race that is set before us, ² looking to Jesus, the founder and perfecter of our faith, who for the joy that was set before him endured the cross, despising the shame, and is seated at the right hand of the throne of God.

Now list everything you learned about angels from these passages.

Though we don't have to correct people or even respond to them when they use the word "angel" to describe someone who has died, it is important to understand the scriptural differences.

There are many examples of God sending angels to do specific tasks for His people in both the Old and New Testaments. You can use your concordance to look up "angels" to find out more about them if you're interested. Jesus said He will send his angels to gather tares out of His kingdom before gathering His wheat into His barn. Studying Bible prophecy will help you understand the Lord's return and the new heavens and earth.

What Are We and What Do We Have in Christ?

If your loved ones who died are not angels…if we're not angels in this world or the next, what is our status? What does the Bible say about believers? You already looked up verses about this in lesson 11. Look back at the list you made of what you are and what you have in Christ. Beloved, these are true for all believers. They are true for you if you are a believer and they are true for your loved ones who are believers.

Read the following passages and note what you learn about your status as a believer.

What We Are / Have in Him	1 JOHN 3:1-2
Whose children are we?	*¹ See what kind of love the Father has given to us, that we should be called children of God; and so we are. The reason why the world does not know us is that it did not know him. ² Beloved, we are God's children now, and what we will be has not yet appeared; but we know that when he appears we shall be like him, because we shall see him as he is.*
What will happen when He appears?	

	1 CORINTHIANS 15:50, 53-58
What do you learn from this passage about the perishable and unperishable?	*⁵⁰ I tell you this, brothers: flesh and blood cannot inherit the kingdom of God, nor does the perishable inherit the imperishable.*
When will death lose its sting?	*⁵³ For this perishable body must put on the imperishable, and this mortal body must put on immortality. ⁵⁴ When the perishable puts on the imperishable, and the mortal puts on immortality, then shall come to pass the saying that is written: "Death is swallowed up in victory." ⁵⁵ "O death, where is your victory? O death, where is your sting?" ⁵⁶ The sting of death is sin,*

What We Are / Have in Him

What do we have in the Lord Jesus Christ?

What should be our response to this truth?

How is God described in verse 4?

What has God done for us (verses 5-6)?

According to verse 4, why did He do this?

What is the result (verse 7)?

How were we saved (verses 8-9)?

and the power of sin is the law. [57] But thanks be to God, who gives us the victory through our Lord Jesus Christ. [58] Therefore, my beloved brothers, be steadfast, immovable, always abounding in the work of the Lord, knowing that in the Lord your labor is not in vain.

EPHESIANS 2:4-9

[4] But God, being rich in mercy, because of the great love with which he loved us, [5] even when we were dead in our trespasses, made us alive together with Christ—by grace you have been saved— [6] and raised us up with him and seated us with him in the heavenly places in Christ Jesus, [7] so that in the coming ages he might show the immeasurable riches of his grace in kindness toward us in Christ Jesus. [8] For by grace you have been saved through faith. And this is not your own doing; it is the gift of God, [9] not a result of works, so that no one may boast.

In addition to what you learned from Ephesians, your list should include all of the following:

You are created in God's image. Genesis 1:26

You are a son of God. Galatians 3:26

You are chosen. Colossians 3:12

You are called, justified and glorified. Romans 8:30

You have been bought with a price. 1 Corinthians 6:20

You are forgiven, cleansed from all unrighteousness. 1 John 1:9

You are marked with a seal, the promised Holy Spirit. Ephesians 1:13

You are a new creation. 2 Corinthians 5:17

You have eternal life. John 3:16

You have access to the Father by one Spirit. Ephesians 2:18

You are a fellow heir with Christ. Romans 8:17

You are called out of darkness into His marvelous light. 1 Peter 2:9

You have been set free from sin and have become a slave of righteousness. Romans 6:17-18

You are the righteousness of God. 2 Corinthians 5:21

You do not have a spirit of fear, but of power, love, and self-control. 2 Timothy 1:7

You are God's temple and His Spirit dwells in you. 1 Corinthians 6:19

You are wonderfully and fearfully made. Psalm 139:14

You can do all things through Him who strengthens you. Philippians 4:13

You are God's workmanship created in Christ to do good works. Ephesians 2:10

You have citizenship in heaven. Philippians 3:20

Beloved, we find the truths from this list so much more exciting than being an angel! We rejoice because of what we have in Christ and who we are in Christ!

Do you know what you have in Christ? Look back over this list. Look up the passages cited and mark them in your Bible so you can find them when you question your position in Christ. Study God's Word and learn what Jesus did for you and what you are in Him!

Just Journaling

In your Journal, complete your list of facts about angels, then add to your list of "What I Learned About God" in the back. Write out verses that touch your heart and give you hope.

Seeking Counsel from Those in Heaven

Dear friend, you may wish you could talk to your loved one, hoping to get their counsel or at least let you know they're okay. But God's Word is clear on the matter: we are not to seek mediums or practice divination ourselves to attempt to communicate with the dead.

Modern culture has made the practice of divination seem harmless. Mediums and witches are in movies and TV shows. They appear to be helpful and kind. But what does God's Word say about such things?

Let's look at some Old Testament passages. Underline *mediums* and note what God says about them and those who turn to them.

Mediums

LEVITICUS 20:6-8

[6] *"If a person turns to mediums and necromancers, whoring after them, I will set my face against that person and will cut him off from among his people.* [7] *Consecrate yourselves, therefore, and be holy, for I am the LORD YOUR GOD.* [8] *Keep my statutes and do them; I am the LORD who sanctifies you.*

DEUTERONOMY 18:10-12

[10] *There shall not be found among you anyone who burns his son or his daughter as an offering, anyone who practices divination or tells fortunes or interprets omens, or a sorcerer* [11] *or a charmer or a medium or a necromancer or one who inquires of the dead,* [12] *for whoever does these things is an abomination to the LORD.*

Why did Saul seek the advice of a medium?

When Samuel appeared, what did he say to Saul? List all that you learn.

1 SAMUEL 28:6-7, 15-19

*⁶ And when Saul inquired of the L*ᴏʀᴅ*, the L*ᴏʀᴅ *did not answer him, either by dreams, or by Urim, or by prophets. ⁷ Then Saul said to his servants, "Seek out for me a woman who is a medium, that I may go to her and inquire of her." And his servants said to him, "Behold, there is a medium at En-dor."*

*¹⁵ Then Samuel said to Saul, "Why have you disturbed me by bringing me up?" Saul answered, "I am in great distress, for the Philistines are warring against me, and God has turned away from me and answers me no more, either by prophets or by dreams. Therefore I have summoned you to tell me what I shall do." ¹⁶ And Samuel said, "Why then do you ask me, since the L*ᴏʀᴅ *has turned from you and become your enemy? ¹⁷ The L*ᴏʀᴅ *has done to you as he spoke by me, for the L*ᴏʀᴅ *has torn the kingdom out of your hand and given it to your neighbor, David. ¹⁸ Because you did not obey the voice of the L*ᴏʀᴅ *and did not carry out his fierce wrath against Amalek, therefore the L*ᴏʀᴅ *has done this thing to you this day. ¹⁹ Moreover, the L*ᴏʀᴅ *will give Israel also with you into the hand of the Philistines, and tomorrow you and your sons shall be with me. The L*ᴏʀᴅ *will give the army of Israel also into the hand of the Philistines."*

What happened to Saul and Why?

1 CHRONICLES 10:13-14

¹³ So Saul died for his breach of faith. He broke faith with the Lᴏʀᴅ in that he did not keep the command of the Lᴏʀᴅ, and also consulted a medium, seeking guidance. ¹⁴ He did not seek guidance from the Lᴏʀᴅ. Therefore, the Lᴏʀᴅ put him to death and turned the kingdom over to David the son of Jesse.

There are many places in the Old Testament where God forbids seeking help from mediums and those who practice divination. Some people say "it's okay to get a reading" if we don't "seek it" or if the medium doesn't charge for services. Some appear to be believers because they prophesy.

Read Acts 16:16-18.

Did proclaiming the truth "These men are the servants of the Most High God" justify what God prohibited?

What did Paul do? Did he address the slave girl?

What can you conclude from this?

ACTS 16:16-18

¹⁶ As we were going to the place of prayer, we were met by a slave girl who had a spirit of divination and brought her owners much gain by fortune-telling. ¹⁷ She followed Paul and us, crying out, "These men are servants of the Most High God, who proclaim to you the way of salvation." ¹⁸ And this she kept doing for many days. Paul, having become greatly annoyed, turned and said to the spirit, "I command you in the name of Jesus Christ to come out of her." And it came out that very hour.

Some even claim that they speak to the dead "in the name of Jesus" which puts a nice spin on it. But according to Acts 19:13-16, "Jewish exorcists" attempted to "invoke the name of the Lord Jesus over those who had evil spirits." One evil spirit attacked them violently.

Read Acts 19: 17-20 to find out how people responded to this violent event.

Note what new believers did with their magic-art books and how expensive (together) they were. What does this tell you about how they valued their new-found faith?

ACTS 19:17-20

17 And this became known to all the residents of Ephesus, both Jews and Greeks. And fear fell upon them all, and the name of the Lord Jesus was extolled. 18 Also many of those who were now believers came, confessing and divulging their practices. 19 And a number of those who had practiced magic arts brought their books together and burned them in the sight of all. And they counted the value of them and found it came to fifty thousand pieces of silver. 20 So the word of the Lord continued to increase and prevail mightily.

Read 1 John 4:1-6 to find out how you can know a spirit is "from God" or not. Underline every mention of *spirit* and note what you learn.

What does the spirit "from God" confess?

What does the spirit "not from God" *not* confess?

Is this spirit neutral? What term tells us it's biased?

Is this spirit coming *only* in the future?

1 JOHN 4:1-6

1 Beloved, do not believe every spirit, but test the spirits to see whether they are from God, for many false prophets have gone out into the world. 2 By this you know the Spirit of God: every spirit that confesses that Jesus Christ has come in the flesh is from God, 3 and every spirit that does not confess Jesus is not from God. This is the spirit of the antichrist, which you heard was coming and now is in the world already.

What's significant about the tense of the term "overcome" (v. 4)? What does "them" refer back to?

Is it more powerful than the God we serve?

If spirits are not from God, what are they "from"?

Why do they have a captive audience? What do they say that is so attractive?

Why will some "listen to us" and others not?

How are the two spirits differentiated in v. 6?

Is there any "in-between," any "gray area" between these two qualities?

⁴ *Little children, you are from God and have overcome them, for he who is in you is greater than he who is in the world.* ⁵ *They are from the world; therefore they speak from the world, and the world listens to them.* ⁶ *We are from God. Whoever knows God listens to us; whoever is not from God does not listen to us. By this we know the Spirit of truth and the spirit of error.*

Review Galatians 5:19-24. Find something in the list of the works of the flesh that relates to our current subject. Look at the terms before and after it.

What are there to "works of the flesh" besides *physical* actions?

GALATIANS 5:19-24

¹⁹ *Now the works of the flesh are evident: sexual immorality, impurity, sensuality,* ²⁰ *idolatry, sorcery, enmity, strife, jealousy, fits of anger, rivalries, dissensions, divisions,* ²¹ *envy, drunkenness, orgies, and things like*

List "the fruit of the Spirit."

these. I warn you, as I warned you before, that those who do such things will not inherit the kingdom of God. ²² But the fruit of the Spirit is love, joy, peace, patience, kindness, goodness, faithfulness, ²³ gentleness, self-control; against such things there is no law. ²⁴ And those who belong to Christ Jesus have crucified the flesh with its passions and desires.

The Lord forbids us to engage mediums, witches, and our own divination to obtain truth, insights, and counsel, whether an attempt to communicate with the dead is made or not.

Who then should we to look to for wisdom? Where is it found?

Read the following passages underlining *wisdom* and marking *inquire, philosophy, empty deceit,* and other key words in distinct ways. Note what you learn about who to inquire from.

Inquiry

ISAIAH 8:19

¹⁹ And when they say to you, "Inquire of the mediums and the necromancers who chirp and mutter," should not a people inquire of their God? Should they inquire of the dead on behalf of the living?

COLOSSIANS 2:6-8

⁶ Therefore, as you received Christ Jesus the Lord, so walk in him, ⁷ rooted and built up in him and established in the faith, just as you were taught,

Inquiry

abounding in thanksgiving. [8] See to it that no one takes you captive by philosophy and empty deceit, according to human tradition, according to the elemental spirits of the world, and not according to Christ.

1 CORINTHIANS 1:18-25

[18] For the word of the cross is folly to those who are perishing, but to us who are being saved it is the power of God. [19] For it is written, "I will destroy the wisdom of the wise, and the discernment of the discerning I will thwart." [20] Where is the one who is wise? Where is the scribe? Where is the debater of this age? Has not God made foolish the wisdom of the world? [21] For since, in the wisdom of God, the world did not know God through wisdom, it pleased God through the folly of what we preach to save those who believe. [22] For Jews demand signs and Greeks seek wisdom, [23] but we preach Christ crucified, a stumbling block to Jews and folly to Gentiles, [24] but to those who are called, both Jews and Greeks, Christ the power of God and the wisdom of God. [25] For the foolishness of God is wiser than men, and the weakness of God is stronger than men.

PSALM 27:13-14

[13] I believe that I shall look upon the goodness of the LORD in the land of the living! [14] Wait for the LORD; be strong, and let your heart take courage; wait for the LORD!

Inquiry

PSALM 25:4-5

⁴ Make me to know your ways, O Lord; teach me your paths. ⁵ Lead me in your truth and teach me, for you are the God of my salvation; for you I wait all the day long.

Heaven may seem far away. You may become impatient waiting for God but look at what happened to King Saul when he *didn't!* Dear one, we must seek wisdom from God; sorcerers, diviners, and mediums don't have it, they're not believers, they don't seek God for these things. We must not trust the wisdom of the world God has made foolish. We are to trust the Lord, not mediums, not angels, not our loved ones who are away from their bodies and at home with Him. They can't protect us or give us wisdom; only God can and does. He promises wisdom to those who seek Him.

If you have solicited a medium to contact the dead or have sought counsel from a witch or diviner, confess your sin and ask God to forgive you. Ask Him to lead you by His Spirit, to help you walk in His Spirit, and to put to death your fleshly desires. Ask Him to help you be patient and wait on Him as He transforms you and gives you comfort. He will help you heal and find true hope, peace, and joy rather than the temporary satisfaction some claim to get from those who allegedly speak to the dead.

JEREMIAH 23:32

Behold, I am against those who prophesy lying dreams, declares the Lord, and who tell them and lead my people astray by their lies and their recklessness, when I did not send them or charge them. So they do not profit this people at all, declares the Lord (see also vv. 16, 27, 28).

Just Journaling

In your Journal, summarize what you learned about seeking counsel from those in heaven.

If you sought the counsel of a sorcerer or medium or if you were or even now are considering it, write what you now know to be true about such things.

LESSON 16

Heaven

In my Father's house are many rooms. If it were not so, would I have told you that I go to prepare a place for you (John 14:2)?

During your grief some friends may have tried to comfort you with "He's in a better place." Is this true? Are our loved ones in a better place? Are they in heaven? These are important questions for those who are grieving. We want to know where our loved ones reside *now* and how they're doing there. However, the Bible does not speak much about what heaven is like before resurrection.

Read Philippians 1:21-23 and 3:20-21 and note what you learn about our condition right after death.

After Death

PHILIPPIANS 1:21-23

21 For to me to live is Christ, and to die is gain. 22 If I am to live in the flesh, that means fruitful labor for me. Yet which I shall choose I cannot tell. 23 I am hard pressed between the two. My desire is to depart and be with Christ, for that is far better

PHILIPPIANS 3:20-21

20 But our citizenship is in heaven, and from it we await a Savior, the Lord Jesus Christ, 21 who will transform our lowly body to be like his glorious body, by the power that enables him even to subject all things to himself.

If being with Christ is "far better," why stay here? Why go on living in this sinful, broken world?

Now read the following passages from Philippians. Mark *suffering*, *loss*, and *gain*, then note what you learn.

Suffering	**PHILIPPIANS 1:24-26, 29-30** *24 But to remain in the flesh is more necessary on your account. 25 Convinced of this, I know that I will remain and continue with you all, for your progress and joy in the faith, 26 so that in me you may have ample cause to glory in Christ Jesus, because of my coming to you again.* *29 For it has been granted to you that for the sake of Christ you should not only believe in him but also suffer for his sake, 30 engaged in the same conflict that you saw I had and now hear that I still have.*
Loss	
	PHILIPPIANS 3:7-11 *7 But whatever gain I had, I counted as loss for the sake of Christ. 8 Indeed, I count everything as loss because of the surpassing worth of knowing Christ Jesus my Lord. For his sake I have suffered the loss of all things and count them as rubbish, in order that I may gain Christ 9 and be found in him, not having a righteousness of my own that comes from the law, but that which comes through faith in Christ, the righteousness from God that depends on faith—10 that I may know him and the power of his resurrection, and may share his sufferings, becoming like him in his death, 11 that by any means possible I may attain the resurrection from the dead.*
Gain	

God revealed to Paul that being with Christ is better than living on earth. He also taught him that the suffering of this world is nothing compared to the glory to come. Paul knew that he still had work to do here on earth. As you read in another lesson, God created us in Christ to do good works which He prepared beforehand (Ephesians 2:10). Beloved, do you consider your current suffering worth what you gain in Christ?

Someone recently said to us "I don't have to decide if my mother's life is worth all that has happened since. Her death happened. I cannot change that. I am grateful for all that God has done in me since her death."

Yes, losing our parents and son has been incredibly hard. Yes, we have grieved much in the past few years. But God has drawn us closer to Him and has done a great work in each of us. Is this work He's doing worth the loss of our parents and son? We don't have to decide that; it's enough to know that the death of the Lord's saints is "precious" to Him (Psalm 116:15). We can't change what happened but we can decide to obey God today. We can choose to think about His good things and be grateful. We can choose to forgive those who harm or offend us. We can choose to live a life that glorifies God now, even in the midst of grief and suffering.

We look forward to heaven for good reasons, particularly our union with Jesus and our reunion with our loved ones. For those who are in Christ, heaven will be wonderful!

Read what Paul wrote in 2 Corinthians 5. Double underline *heaven (heavens, heavenly, etc.)*. Underline references to our *earthly body* including *earthly home* and *this tent*. Circle *building from God*. Note what you learn in the chart that follows.

2 CORINTHIANS 5:1-10

¹ *For we know that if the tent that is our earthly home is destroyed, we have a building from God, a house not made with hands, eternal in the heavens.* ² *For in this tent we groan, longing to put on our heavenly dwelling,* ³ *if indeed by putting it on we may not be found naked.* ⁴ *For while we are still in this tent, we groan, being burdened—not that we would be unclothed, but that we would be further clothed, so that what is mortal may be swallowed up by life.* ⁵ *He who has prepared us for this very thing is God, who has given us the Spirit as a guarantee.* ⁶ *So we are always of good courage. We know that while we are at home in the body we are away from the Lord,* ⁷ *for we walk by faith, not by*

sight. ⁸ Yes, we are of good courage, and we would rather be away from the
body and at home with the Lord. ⁹ So whether we are at home or away, we
make it our aim to please him. ¹⁰ For we must all appear before the judgment
seat of Christ, so that each one may receive what is due for what he has done in
the body, whether good or evil.

Now complete this chart. Write everything you learn from this passage about
our earthly and heavenly bodies.

Earthly Body	**Heavenly Body**

According to verses 6-9, what should our aim here on earth be? How should
we live today?

According to verse 10, where must everyone appear? Why?

Even when we have a wonderful life, to be with Christ is better than living on
earth. Heaven *is* a better place. If our loved ones were Christians they are at
home with the Lord in heaven, which is a beautiful thing! But we are still on
earth and have good work to do. God in His infinite wisdom has chosen to
have us continue to live here. How does this make you feel?

Just Journaling

What are you feeling about what you just learned? How are you living up to
what you read in Philippians and 2 Corinthians? Write about it and ask God
to help you apply these truths in your life.

Also in your Journal, list everything you learned about heaven. Add to this list as you study the rest of this lesson.

What Is Heaven Like?

Four men in Scripture saw visions of heaven: Isaiah, Ezekiel, John, and a man mentioned by Paul in 2 Corinthians. When they wrote what they had seen and/ or heard, God's majesty was the focus. (You may want to study the books of Ezekiel, Isaiah, and Revelation to learn more about the visions of these men.)

Read 2 Corinthians 11:30-33, 12:1-5, 9-10 and note what you learn about heaven.

Heaven

2 CORINTHIANS 11:30-33, 12:1-5, 9-10

[30] *If I must boast, I will boast of the things that show my weakness.* [31] *The God and Father of the Lord Jesus, he who is blessed forever, knows that I am not lying.* [32] *At Damascus, the governor under King Aretas was guarding the city of Damascus in order to seize me,* [33] *but I was let down in a basket through a window in the wall and escaped his hands.*

[12:1] *I must go on boasting. Though there is nothing to be gained by it, I will go on to visions and revelations of the Lord.* [2] *I know a man in Christ who fourteen years ago was caught up to the third heaven—whether in the body or out of the body I do not know, God knows.* [3] *And I know that this man was caught up into paradise—whether in the body or out of the body I do not know, God knows—* [4] *and he heard things that cannot be told, which man may not utter.* [5] *On behalf of this man I will boast, but on my own behalf I will not boast, except of my weaknesses*

What does Paul choose to boast in? In other words, what is his focus?

⁹But he said to me, "My grace is sufficient for you, for my power is made perfect in weakness." Therefore I will boast all the more gladly of my weaknesses, so that the power of Christ may rest upon me. ¹⁰For the sake of Christ, then, I am content with weaknesses, insults, hardships, persecutions, and calamities. For when I am weak, then I am strong.

What do you learn about weakness from this passage?

How can you apply this in your grief?

What about you, my friend? Are you experiencing God's grace and power in your weaknesses, in your grief today?

Isaiah wrote about a Holy One seated on a throne and his low unholy condition by contrast. His view of himself was: "Woe is me! For I am lost; for I am a man of unclean lips and I dwell in the midst of a people of unclean lips; for my eyes have seen the King, the LORD of hosts!" (Isaiah 6:5).

Now read the rest of Isaiah 6:1-8 and note what you learn about what Isaiah saw in his vision.

Describe what Isaiah saw.

ISAIAH 6:1-8

¹In the year that King Uzziah died I saw the Lord sitting upon a throne, high and lifted up; and the train of his robe filled the temple. ²Above him stood the seraphim. Each had six wings: with two he covered his face, and with two he covered his feet, and with two he flew. ³And one called to another and said: "Holy, holy, holy is the LORD of hosts; the

What happened after he confessed his uncleanness?

How did he respond to what happened?

whole earth is full of his glory!" [4] *And the foundations of the thresholds shook at the voice of him who called, and the house was filled with smoke.* [5] *And I said: "Woe is me! For I am lost; for I am a man of unclean lips, and I dwell in the midst of a people of unclean lips; for my eyes have seen the King, the LORD of hosts!"* [6] *Then one of the seraphim flew to me, having in his hand a burning coal that he had taken with tongs from the altar.* [7] *And he touched my mouth and said: "Behold, this has touched your lips; your guilt is taken away, and your sin atoned for."* [8] *And I heard the voice of the Lord saying, "Whom shall I send, and who will go for us?" Then I said, "Here I am! Send me."*

John wrote in Revelation 4:1, "After this I looked, and behold, a door standing open in heaven! And the first voice, which I had heard speaking to me like a trumpet, said, 'Come up here, and I will show you what must take place after this.'" He went on to describe God seated on a throne.

Read Revelation 4:6-11 and note how John describes heaven.

Heaven	**REVELATION 4:6-11**
	[6]*and before the throne there was as it were a sea of glass, like crystal.*
	And around the throne, on each side of the throne, are four living creatures, full of eyes in front and behind: [7]*the first living creature like a lion, the second living creature like an ox, the third living creature with the face of a man, and the fourth living creature like an eagle in flight.* [8]*And the four living creatures, each of them with six wings, are full of eyes all around and*

Heaven

within, and day and night they never cease to say, "Holy, holy, holy, is the Lord God Almighty, who was and is and is to come!" [9] And whenever the living creatures give glory and honor and thanks to him who is seated on the throne, who lives forever and ever, [10] the twenty-four elders fall down before him who is seated on the throne and worship him who lives forever and ever. They cast their crowns before the throne, saying, [11] "Worthy are you, our Lord and God, to receive glory and honor and power, for you created all things, and by your will they existed and were created."

Jesus said that He was going to heaven to prepare a place for those who believe in Him. Read John 14:1-7 and list what you learn about heaven.

Heaven

JOHN 14:1-7

[1] "Let not your hearts be troubled. Believe in God; believe also in me. [2] In my Father's house are many rooms. If it were not so, would I have told you that I go to prepare a place for you? [3] And if I go and prepare a place for you, I will come again and will take you to myself, that where I am you may be also. [4] And you know the way to where I am going." [5] Thomas said to him, "Lord, we do not know where you are going. How can we know the way?" [6] Jesus said to him, "I am the way, and the truth, and the life. No one comes to the Father except through me. [7] If you had known me, you would have known my Father also. From now on you do know him and have seen him."

According to verse 6, how does anyone get to the Father?

Peter tells us there also will be new heavens and a new earth in which righteousness dwells. We don't have time to look at this in-depth, so you may want to do a study of heaven in the book of Revelation on your own. For now, let's get an idea of what the new heavens and earth will be like from a few verses.

Read Revelation 21:1-4 and 22:1-5 and note what is promised to us. What will the new heavens and earth be like one day?

The New Heavens and Earth

REVELATION 21:1-4

¹ Then I saw a new heaven and a new earth, for the first heaven and the first earth had passed away, and the sea was no more. ² And I saw the holy city, new Jerusalem, coming down out of heaven from God, prepared as a bride adorned for her husband. ³ And I heard a loud voice from the throne saying, "Behold, the dwelling place of God is with man. He will dwell with them, and they will be his people, and God himself will be with them as their God. ⁴ He will wipe away every tear from their eyes, and death shall be no more, neither shall there be mourning, nor crying, nor pain anymore, for the former things have passed away."

REVELATION 22:1-5

¹ Then the angel showed me the river of the water of life, bright as crystal, flowing from the throne of God and of the Lamb ² through the middle of the street of the city; also, on either side of the river, the tree of life with its twelve kinds of fruit, yielding its fruit each month. The leaves of the tree were for the healing of the nations. ³ No longer will there be anything accursed, but the

The New Heavens and Earth

throne of God and of the Lamb will be in it, and his servants will worship him. ⁴ They will see his face, and his name will be on their foreheads. ⁵ And night will be no more. They will need no light of lamp or sun, for the Lord God will be their light, and they will reign forever and ever.

Doesn't this sound wonderful? No more death, mourning, crying or pain! No more darkness, just Light! Yes, heaven will be glorious. It will be wonderful to see our loved ones again, but how much more wonderful to see God in all His Glory—to see Him as He is and worship Him at His throne! My friend, THAT is something to look forward to!

Many bereaved people we know say they think more about heaven than they did before. When people we love die we begin to seriously consider heaven and our own future. We tend to think about what heaven will be like and wonder what our loved ones are doing there. We know that we "now see in a mirror dimly" but one day it will be "face to face." As Paul adds, "Now I know in part; then I shall know fully, even as I have been fully known" (1 Corinthians 13:12). We look forward to joining our loved ones in heaven someday, but for now, we live here on earth.

Summarize what you have learned about heaven from these passages. How have your thoughts about heaven changed?

Just Journaling

Add anything you learned to your list "Heaven." Write what you are thinking and feeling about heaven.

Who Goes to Heaven?

Are our loved ones in heaven? Are they okay?

If your departed loved ones are Christians, they are with the Lord and okay. Earlier in this lesson, you looked at 2 Corinthians 5:1-5 and Philippians 1:21-23. These passages make it clear that being in the presence of Christ is better than life on earth. When Christians die, when "our earthly home is destroyed, we have a building from God, a house not made with hands, eternal in the heavens."

How can we know if our loved one is a Christian? We cannot know a person's heart. We cannot know for certain who is saved (a true believer) and who is not; that is between each person and the Lord. God sees the heart of man. But we can look at the lives of people to see if they are bearing the fruit of the Spirit and appear to be walking with the Lord (Matthew 7:15-23), and that may bring some comfort.

Read Matthew 7:15-23. Underline *false prophets* and *tree that does not bear fruit*. Double underline *healthy tree*. Note what you learn about fruit.

Fruit

What do you learn about those who do not bear fruit?

MATTHEW 7:15-23

[15] *"Beware of false prophets, who come to you in sheep's clothing but inwardly are ravenous wolves.* [16] *You will recognize them by their fruits. Are grapes gathered from thornbushes, or figs from thistles?* [17] *So, every healthy tree bears good fruit, but the diseased tree bears bad fruit.* [18] *A healthy tree cannot bear bad fruit, nor can a diseased tree bear good fruit.* [19] *Every tree that does not bear good fruit is cut down and thrown into the fire.* [20] *Thus you will recognize them by their fruits.* [21] *"Not everyone who says to me, 'Lord, Lord,' will enter the kingdom of heaven, but the one who does the will of my Father who is in heaven.* [22] *On that day many will say to me, 'Lord, Lord,*

What will happen to them?

did we not prophesy in your name, and cast out demons in your name, and do many mighty works in your name?' [23] *And then will I declare to them, 'I never knew you; depart from me, you workers of lawlessness.'*

While we may not be certain about the salvation of other people, dear one, you can know if *you* are saved. You can know if *you* are going to heaven when you die. The entire book of 1 John is the classic for assurance of salvation. Here are some relevant passages from that book and from others.

Read the passages and mark all time phrases. Draw a triangle over *God* and all synonyms that refer to Him. Draw a cross over every reference to *Jesus* and *Son of Man*. Underline *saved, justified,* and *reconciled*. Note what you learn about the characteristics of true believers.

True Believers' Characteristics

JOHN 3:14-18

[14] *And as Moses lifted up the serpent in the wilderness, so must the Son of Man be lifted up,* [15] *that whoever believes in him may have eternal life.* [16] *"For God so loved the world, that he gave his only Son, that whoever believes in him should not perish but have eternal life.* [17] *For God did not send his Son into the world to condemn the world, but in order that the world might be saved through him.* [18] *Whoever believes in him is not condemned, but whoever does not believe is condemned already, because he has not believed in the name of the only Son of God.*

ROMANS 5:6-11

[6] *For while we were still weak, at the right time Christ died for the ungodly.* [7] *For one will scarcely die for a righteous person—though perhaps for a good*

True Believers' Characteristics

person one would dare even to die—[8] but God shows his love for us in that while we were still sinners, Christ died for us. [9] Since, therefore, we have now been justified by his blood, much more shall we be saved by him from the wrath of God. [10] For if while we were enemies we were reconciled to God by the death of his Son, much more, now that we are reconciled, shall we be saved by his life. [11] More than that, we also rejoice in God through our Lord Jesus Christ, through whom we have now received reconciliation.

ROMANS 10:8-10

[8] But what does it say? "The word is near you, in your mouth and in your heart" (that is, the word of faith that we proclaim); [9] because, if you confess with your mouth that Jesus is Lord and believe in your heart that God raised him from the dead, you will be saved. [10] For with the heart one believes and is justified, and with the mouth one confesses and is saved.

1 JOHN 1:5-10

[5] This is the message we have heard from him and proclaim to you, that God is light, and in him is no darkness at all. [6] If we say we have fellowship with him while we walk in darkness, we lie and do not practice the truth. [7] But if we walk in the light, as he is in the light, we have fellowship with one another, and the blood of Jesus his Son cleanses us from all sin. [8] If we say we have no sin, we deceive ourselves, and

True Believers' Characteristics

the truth is not in us. ⁹ *If we confess our sins, he is faithful and just to forgive us our sins and to cleanse us from all unrighteousness.* ¹⁰ *If we say we have not sinned, we make him a liar, and his word is not in us.*

1 JOHN 2:4-6

⁴ *Whoever says "I know him" but does not keep his commandments is a liar, and the truth is not in him,* ⁵ *but whoever keeps his word, in him truly the love of God is perfected. By this we may know that we are in him:* ⁶ *whoever says he abides in him ought to walk in the same way in which he walked.*

Summarize what you learned about salvation, justification, and reconciliation.

From what you have studied, how can you know if you are a Christian?

If you have not confessed Jesus and are not sure if you will go to heaven, today is the day of salvation! Read the passages again. Review what you have learned about God in this study. Pray and tell God what you are thinking and feeling.

If you have confessed Jesus but still lack assurance of your eternal life, read 1 John, which was written so we can know we have eternal life. If after reading this letter God reveals to you that you are not His child, confess Him now.

One last topic . . .

Parents who have lost a child want to know, "Do preborn babies, infants, and young children go to heaven?" Unfortunately, this is a topic the Bible does not address directly and traditions vary. Read the following passages and see what you learn.

Children and Heaven

2 SAMUEL 12:16, 22-23

[16] *David therefore sought God on behalf of the child. And David fasted and went in and lay all night on the ground.*

[22] *He said, "While the child was still alive, I fasted and wept, for I said, 'Who knows whether the LORD will be gracious to me, that the child may live?'* [23] *But now he is dead. Why should I fast? Can I bring him back again? I shall go to him, but he will not return to me."*

MATTHEW 19:13-15

[13] *Then children were brought to him that he might lay his hands on them and pray. The disciples rebuked the people,* [14] *but Jesus said, "Let the little children come to me and do not hinder them, for to such belongs the kingdom of heaven."* [15] *And he laid his hands on them and went away.*

1 TIMOTHY 2:4-6

[4] *who desires all people to be saved and to come to the knowledge of the truth.* [5] *For there is one God, and there is one mediator between God and men, the man Christ Jesus,* [6] *who gave himself as a ransom for all, which is the testimony given at the proper time.*

Children and Heaven

2 PETER 3:9

⁹ The Lord is not slow to fulfill his promise as some count slowness, but is patient toward you, not wishing that any should perish, but that all should reach repentance.

COLOSSIANS 1:15-20

¹⁵ He is the image of the invisible God, the firstborn of all creation. ¹⁶ For by him all things were created, in heaven and on earth, visible and invisible, whether thrones or dominions or rulers or authorities—all things were created through him and for him. ¹⁷ And he is before all things, and in him all things hold together. ¹⁸ And he is the head of the body, the church. He is the beginning, the firstborn from the dead, that in everything he might be preeminent. ¹⁹ For in him all the fullness of God was pleased to dwell, ²⁰ and through him to reconcile to himself all things, whether on earth or in heaven, making peace by the blood of his cross.

The Bible does not clearly state whether preborn and infant children can understand the gospel or just go to heaven apart from faith. We do know that God's nature is love and that He is merciful, righteous, and just.

From what you have read in these passages and what you have learned about God and heaven, what do you think?

Just Journaling

In your Journal, summarize what you learned about who goes to heaven and who does not.

If you are a Christian, take time to write out your testimony regarding when you became a believer.

If you are not a Christian, write about that.

LESSON 17

How Then Shall We Live?

The death of my child changed me
I am forever changed
But death does not define me

It is no longer I who live, but Christ who lives in me (Galatians 2:20).

The death of a loved one changes us. We no longer live with the fantasy that bad things don't happen. We know they do! We are wounded and hurting. Our theology has been shaken to its core. We are changed in ways we can't express and others who have not experienced such loss can't understand.

However, the deep suffering and grief we have over the loss of a loved one do not entitle us to ignore God's commands in His Word, and they shouldn't because these very commands are for our own good, our relief, short-term and long-term. As we saw in Psalm 119 God's Word is life! If it's not our delight, we will perish in our affliction. We must never forget His precepts but always obey them, for through them He has given us life: "Of His own will He brought us forth by the Word of truth" (James 1:18). Rather than choosing self-reliance based on the flawed values of this world, we must choose true life!

We've found that we need to work out our salvation with fear and trembling (Philippians 2:12-13) even more when we're suffering. We need to know that God is working in us both to will and work His good pleasure. When we're suffering we cling to the truth of His Word for our own sanity and for our life.

How do we "work out" our salvation? How do we live well while we grieve?

PHILIPPIANS 2:12-13

12 Therefore, my beloved, as you have always obeyed, so now, not only as in my presence but much more in my absence, work out your own salvation with fear and trembling, 13 for it is God who works in you, both to will and to work for his good pleasure.

The book of James gives us lots of instruction on how to live while suffering. We looked at a few verses from James already but we're going to look at them more closely in this lesson. This book can be especially helpful to us who grieve as we walk through our trials. Suffering and trials are two of its recurring themes; we learn how to behave as followers of Jesus and how to treat others while we grieve. And we can find healing and peace as we apply these truths in our lives.

James 1:2 highlights *when* you meet trials of various kinds, not *if*. Read James 1:2-4, 12-15. Underline the words *trials, testing,* and *temptation* along with any synonyms. Circle the word *steadfastness* and mark any other key phrases that instruct you how to live during trials.

Living Through Trials

JAMES 1:2-4, 12-15

Do you want to be perfect and complete, not lacking anything? How can you realize such things?

2 Count it all joy, my brothers, when you meet trials of various kinds, 3 for you know that the testing of your faith produces steadfastness. 4 And let steadfastness have its full effect, that you may be perfect and complete, lacking in nothing.

According to verse 12 what will happen to the one who is steadfast?

What do verses 12-15 teach about temptation?

12 Blessed is the man who remains steadfast under trial, for when he has stood the test he will receive the crown of life, which God has promised to those who love him. 13 Let no one say when he is tempted, "I am being tempted by God," for God cannot be tempted with evil, and he himself tempts no one. 14 But each person is tempted when he is lured and enticed by his own desire. 15 Then desire when it has conceived gives birth to sin, and sin when it is fully grown brings forth death.

Now read 1 Corinthians 10:12-13. Note what you learn.

Living Through Trials

1 CORINTHIANS 10:12-13

[12] Therefore let anyone who thinks that he stands take heed lest he fall. [13] No temptation has overtaken you that is not common to man. God is faithful, and he will not let you be tempted beyond your ability, but with the temptation he will also provide the way of escape, that you may be able to endure it.

Read James 1:16-18. Draw a triangle over every reference to *the Father* and all synonyms that refer to Him. Note what you learn about God here and in your *Journal.*

God

JAMES 1:16-18

[16] Do not be deceived, my beloved brothers. [17] Every good gift and every perfect gift is from above, coming down from the Father of lights with whom there is no variation or shadow due to change. [18] Of his own will he brought us forth by the word of truth, that we should be a kind of firstfruits of his creatures.

Just Journaling

In your journal, summarize what you learned about trials, temptation, and suf-fering from James 1 and 1 Corinthians 10. Here, write out one recent trial you know the Lord brought you through.

As you have gone through this study, what ways have you seen God working through your grief, through the trials and suffering you have faced? Have you had temptations in your grief? How did you handle them?

Just Journaling

Have you been changed by the death of someone you love? Can you list the ways you have been changed? List both good and bad ways you see yourself changed. Ask God to show you anything you missed. Be honest in your assessment.

For the rest of this lesson we are going to look at some of the instructions James gives to dispersed believers along with some cross-references. These instructions are for us today, my friend. They tell us how we can live in our suffering as we go through trials. Let us learn together how to live according to the Spirit even in the midst of grief.

Wisdom

Do you need wisdom in dealing with others in your life? Do you need wisdom to know how to deal with all your emotions and grief? It is work to seek God and study His Word. It is work to gain wisdom and apply it in our lives. But, dear one, the work is worth the reward!

Read this passage from Proverbs and shade the word *wisdom* and all synonyms. Then list all you learn about wisdom.

Wisdom	PROVERBS 1:1-7
	¹ The proverbs of Solomon, son of David, king of Israel: ² To know wisdom and instruction, to understand words of insight, ³ to receive instruction in wise dealing, in righteousness, justice, and equity; ⁴ to give prudence to the simple, knowledge and discretion to the youth—⁵ Let the wise hear and increase in learning, and the one who understands obtain guidance, ⁶ to understand a proverb and a saying, the words of the wise and their riddles. ⁷ The fear of the LORD is the beginning of knowledge; fools despise wisdom and instruction.

From this passage we learn that we should desire and seek wisdom. But where do we find it? How do we get wisdom? Read these passages from James 1 and shade the word *wisdom* and all synonyms. Then list all that you learn.

Wisdom	**JAMES 1:5-8**
Who gives wisdom?	*5 If any of you lacks wisdom, let him ask God, who gives generously to all without reproach, and it will be given him. 6 But let him ask in faith, with no doubting, for the one who doubts is like a wave of the sea that is driven and tossed by the wind. 7 For that person must not suppose that he will receive anything from the Lord; 8 he is a double-minded man, unstable in all his ways.*
What is required to obtain wisdom?	
If we don't meet this condition, what are we and how does it impact our behaviors?	

JAMES 3:13-18

13 Who is wise and understanding among you? By his good conduct let him show his works in the meekness of wisdom. 14 But if you have bitter jealousy and selfish ambition in your hearts, do not boast and be false to the truth. 15 This is not the wisdom that comes down from above, but is earthly, unspiritual, demonic. 16 For where jealousy and selfish ambition exist, there will be disorder and every vile practice. 17 But the wisdom from above is first pure, then peaceable, gentle, open to reason, full of mercy and good fruits, impartial and sincere. 18 And a harvest of righteousness is sown in peace by those who make peace.

According to verse 13 what are the wise and understanding told to do?

Contrast the two kinds of "wisdom" in this passage.

Earthly Wisdom	**Wisdom From Above**

Do you have some of each wisdom? Which one prevails in your life? Which one will help you heal in your grief?

Do you have anything you need to talk to God about regarding bitter jealousy or selfish ambition? Pray. Confess your sin. Ask God to show you a better way to live. Ask Him for wisdom from above.

Controlling Our Tongue

Controlling our tongue is hard even when we're feeling great and life is going our way. But it's nearly impossible when we're grieving! Yet that is exactly when we need to do it. We need the help of the Holy Spirit to control our words when we're hurting. Let's look at what James has to say about our words.

In these passages draw a box around the words *tongue* and *speak* and all synonyms. Underline any instructions regarding your behavior and speech.

How We Should Speak

What are we to "put away"?

JAMES 1:19-21

19 Know this, my beloved brothers: let every person be quick to hear, slow to speak, slow to anger; 20 for the anger of man does not produce the righteousness of God. 21 Therefore put away all filthiness and rampant wickedness and receive with meekness the implanted word, which is able to save your souls

JAMES 1:26

26 If anyone thinks he is religious and does not bridle his tongue but deceives his heart, this person's religion is worthless.

JAMES 3:2, 5-10

2 For we all stumble in many ways. And if anyone does not stumble in what he says, he is a perfect man, able also to bridle his whole body.

5 So also the tongue is a small member, yet it boasts of great things. How great a forest is set ablaze by such a small fire! 6 And the tongue is a fire, a world of unrighteousness. The tongue is set among our members, staining the whole body, setting on fire the entire course of life, and set on fire by hell. 7 For every kind of beast and bird, of reptile and sea creature, can be tamed and has been tamed by mankind, 8 but no human being can tame the tongue.

According to verses 9-10 what do "we" do that we shouldn't?

It is a restless evil, full of deadly poison. ⁹ With it we bless our Lord and Father, and with it we curse people who are made in the likeness of God. ¹⁰ From the same mouth come blessing and cursing. My brothers, these things ought not to be so.

How can you "bridle" the tongue you have by birth (cf. 1:19, 26; 3:2)?

How can you use the tongue you have by rebirth (Ephesians 4:15; Colossians 4:6)?

In Lesson 13 we learned about forgiveness. We studied God's commands to forgive others. Have you forgiven those who have hurt you in your suffering? Are you constantly talking about what they did to you? If so, are you cursing them with your tongue? Think through this and ask God to show you anything you need to change, how to apply this truth in your life as you grieve.

Now read James 4:11-12, 2:12-13 and 5:9. Mark *tongue* and *speak* in a distinct way. Underline instructions regarding your speech and how to treat others.

Speech Warnings

JAMES 4:11-12

¹¹ Do not speak evil against one another, brothers. The one who speaks against a brother or judges his brother, speaks evil against the law and judges the law. But if you judge the law, you are not a doer of the law but a judge. ¹² There is only one lawgiver and judge, he who is able to save and to destroy. But who are you to judge your neighbor?

Speech Warnings

JAMES 2:12-13

¹² *So speak and so act as those who are to be judged under the law of liberty.* ¹³ *For judgment is without mercy to one who has shown no mercy. Mercy triumphs over judgment.*

JAMES 5:9

⁹ *Do not grumble against one another, brothers, so that you may not be judged; behold, the Judge is standing at the door.*

What have you learned about bridling the tongue of flesh? Summarize what you learned.

It's hard to speak kindly to others when we're hurting but, my friend, grief is not an excuse to be mean or harsh with our tongues. Look back at James 2:12-13. Are you showing mercy to others? Are you speaking as one who will be judged under the law of liberty or "without mercy"? Have you been grumbling against others?

Do you need to confess anything or talk to God about your speech? Take time to do that now.

Just Journaling

Summarize in your Journal what you learned about wisdom and bridling your tongue. Then confess anything you need to confess to God. Write a prayer of confession and ask God to show you how and help you change.

Be Doers of the Word: Faith & Works

When we are mourning, in the days of deep grief, we don't want to get up and do stuff. We may want to lay around or sit and sob. But does being controlled by our pain over the long-term bring glory to God? Will we find healing if we spend years in darkness and sorrow, weeping over our loss rather than living the life God has given us today? Beloved, as you grieve, can you do what God has called you to do? As Ephesians 2:10 says, "we are his workmanship, created in Christ Jesus for good works, which God prepared beforehand, that we should walk in them."

Read the following passages and underline *the word* and any synonyms. Circle *perseveres*. Draw a triangle over references to *God*. Underline any instructions. List any commands and note what you learn.

Commands

JAMES 1:22-25

²² But be doers of the word, and not hearers only, deceiving yourselves. ²³ For if anyone is a hearer of the word and not a doer, he is like a man who looks intently at his natural face in a mirror. ²⁴ For he looks at himself and goes away and at once forgets what he was like. ²⁵ But the one who looks into the perfect law, the law of liberty, and perseveres, being no hearer who forgets but a doer who acts, he will be blessed in his doing.

JAMES 1:27

²⁷Religion that is pure and undefiled before God, the Father, is this: to visit orphans and widows in their affliction, and to keep oneself unstained from the world.

JAMES 2:14-17

¹⁴ What good is it, my brothers, if someone says he has faith but does not have works? Can that faith save him? ¹⁵ If a brother or sister is poorly clothed and lacking in daily food, ¹⁶ and one of you says to them, "Go in peace, be warmed and filled," without giving them the things needed for the body, what good is that? ¹⁷ So also faith by itself, if it does not have works, is dead.

What do you learn about faith from James 2:15-17?

Is James saying we must add works to dead faith to be saved or is he saying that living faith generates works by definition? (Note v. 17's "have".)

Early in your grief, did you have friends and family visit you and bring you food or other gifts? How did these visits and gifts help you?

Are you willing to help others in similar ways now? Is there a family in your church that is struggling, perhaps one that recently added a child through birth or adoption? Would you consider taking a meal to them? Would you be willing to fold laundry or help with yard work?

My friend, put your faith into action by helping others this week. This may *seem* hard . . . because *it is!* It's hard to reach out to help others when we ourselves are hurting. But God knows this is part of our healing. He knows what is best for us because He is a loving Father. He wants to transform you as you heal in your grief.

Just Journaling

In your Journal, summarize what you learned about "doing" the Word. Then start a list of ways you can help others. After that, look for creative ways to do these things.

Wait Patiently and Do What Is Right

As mentioned in an earlier lesson, patience is difficult when we're suffering. We want an end to our pain, NOW! Yet God tells us to patiently wait for our full transformation into the image of His Son. As He molds and makes us into the person He wants us to be, we must trust Him and be patient. We must wait for the day of His coming when we'll be confirmed blameless before Him.

In the following passages underline *suffering* and circle the words *patient, patience,* and *steadfast.* Mark all time references. Mark other keywords as you have been doing in this lesson. Note what you learn about patience.

Patience

What does James command in verses 7-8?

What examples of this disposition does he give in verses 10 and 11?

What does this passage say about those who are steadfast and patient?

Now read James 4:13-17.

JAMES 5:7-8, 10-11

[7] Be patient, therefore, brothers, until the coming of the Lord. See how the farmer waits for the precious fruit of the earth, being patient about it, until it receives the early and the late rains. [8] You also, be patient. Establish your hearts, for the coming of the Lord is at hand. [10] As an example of suffering and patience, brothers, take the prophets who spoke in the name of the Lord. [11] Behold, we consider those blessed who remained steadfast. You have heard of the steadfastness of Job, and you have seen the purpose of the Lord, how the Lord is compassionate and merciful.

JAMES 4:13-17

[13] Come now, you who say, "Today or tomorrow we will go into such and such a town and spend a year there and trade and make a profit"—[14] yet you do not know what tomorrow will bring. What is your life? For you are a mist that appears for a little time and then vanishes. [15] Instead you ought to say, "If the Lord wills, we will live and do this or that." [16] As it is, you boast in your arrogance. All such boasting is evil. [17] So whoever knows the right thing to do and fails to do it, for him it is sin.[1]

If you are reading this book, you have probably lost a loved one and already know that life is a mist.

---

[1] The book of James is a wonderful guidebook for how we are to live and persevere during trials and suffering. Consider joining a local or online Precept Ministries class to study this insightful book.

How does this make you feel?

What does this passage teach about boasting about the future? What should our perspective be and why?

We who have lost loved ones understand clearly that this life is a mist that appears for a little time and then vanishes. We know we're not promised tomorrow. But James tells us that we must still do the right thing. We should wait patiently for the coming of the Lord.

Beloved, are there right things you know you should be doing? Have you mistreated others while you grieve? Have you neglected prayer and Bible study? Have your emotions controlled your actions rather than the Spirit? Have you spent your time with your mind set on things of the flesh instead of things of the Spirit? If so, confess your sin to God and ask Him to help you change.

God loves you. He has given us His Holy Word so that we can know how to live in peace with joy. He has set us free from the bondage of weak and worthless things of this world. Will you choose to be led by the Spirit and walk in the Spirit? We pray that you will.

Just Journaling

Are you waiting patiently for the coming of the Lord? Write what is going on with you today. How are you handling your grief today? Are you seeing the good that God is doing in you as you seek Him, study His Word and apply truth in your life?

LESSON 18

Bless the Lord, O My Soul

[Kathleen] Years ago, I memorized Psalm 103 with our children as part of our school curriculum. At the time it was simply something to memorize and recite like a poem or speech. But eventually God revealed to me that His Word is Truth from cover to cover. From that point on, as I meditated on this passage God brought me great comfort.

When I lost my dad one Easter morning, this passage came to my mind. Two years later as I sat in the hospital room with my dying father-in-law, and even later as I cared for my mother-in-law as she was dying from cancer, the words of this passage comforted me.

The morning that I learned our son was dead, again it was this passage that came first to my mind:

> **Bless the LORD, O my soul,**
> **and all that is within me,**
> **bless his holy name!**
> **Bless the LORD, O my soul,**
> **and forget not all his benefits,**
> **The LORD is merciful and gracious,**
> **slow to anger and abounding in steadfast love.**
> **(Psalm 103:1-2, 8)**

Even though I was hurting terribly over the loss of our son I knew from studying the Bible that God is compassionate, gracious, and abounding in steadfast love. I knew that He was still with me and would take care of me. I'm so grateful that Scripture is Truth. I'm grateful that I do not have to rely on my feelings to know God and what He has done for me.

In my grief my feelings told me to give up because everything was horrible! My life would never be the same again! My feelings told me nothing would ever be okay again! My feelings lied to me. God's Word tells us that He is wonderful and worthy of our praise! God's Word tells us that He has compassion on His children. He is worthy of praise, even as we grieve. God's Word can be trusted; it is truth.

As you walk through your grief journey, you will have times of deep sadness and times when your emotions cause you to doubt God. Studying His Word and understanding what it says will help you stand up to the doubts and fears common in grief.

For our last lesson let's look at three passages that will bring you strength and comfort in your grief: Psalms 103 and 23 plus John 10.

Psalm 103

Many psalms are laments and they are full of truth about God. Reading and studying the psalms in your grief will bring you comfort and lead to healing and peace as you apply what you learn about God in your life. Read Psalm 103 on these next pages. Mark important phrases in a distinct way. Be sure to mark every mention of *Lord* including synonyms and pronouns that refer to Him.

PSALM 103
Of David.

Who is David speaking to? What does he advise?

¹ *Bless the* Lord, *O my soul,*
    and all that is within me,
        bless his holy name!
² *Bless the* Lord, *O my soul,*
    and forget not all his benefits,

What are God's benefits?

³ *who forgives all your iniquity,*
    who heals all your diseases,
⁴ *who redeems your life from the pit,*
    who crowns you with steadfast love
        and mercy,
⁵ *who satisfies you with good*
    so that your youth is renewed like
        the eagle's.
⁶ *The* Lord *works righteousness*
    and justice for all who are
        oppressed.

How is God described?

What is God's attitude towards our sin?

What is our life here on earth like?

What's God's attitude towards those who fear Him and keep His covenant? Does His love for us end when we die?

7 He made known his ways to Moses,
his acts to the people of Israel.
8 The Lord *is merciful and gracious,*
slow to anger and abounding in
steadfast love.
9 He will not always chide,
nor will he keep his anger forever.
10 He does not deal with us according to
our sins,
nor repay us according to our
iniquities.
11 For as high as the heavens are above
the earth,
so great is his steadfast love toward
those who fear him;
12 as far as the east is from the west,
so far does he remove our
transgressions from us.
13 As a father shows compassion to his
children,
so the Lord *shows compassion to*
those who fear him.
14 For he knows our frame;
he remembers that we are dust.
15 As for man, his days are like grass;
he flourishes like a flower of the
field;
16 for the wind passes over it, and it is
gone,
and its place knows it no more.
17 But the steadfast love of the Lord *is*
from everlasting to everlasting on
those who fear him,
and his righteousness to children's
children,
18 to those who keep his covenant
and remember to do his
commandments.

What is the extent of God's sovereignty?	_¹⁹ The Lᴏʀᴅ has established his throne in the heavens, and his kingdom rules over all._
Who does the Psalmist call to bless the Lord?	_²⁰ Bless the Lᴏʀᴅ, O you his angels, you mighty ones who do his word, obeying the voice of his word! ²¹ Bless the Lᴏʀᴅ, all his hosts, his ministers, who do his will!_
How does David wrap up this psalm?	_²² Bless the Lᴏʀᴅ, all his works, in all places of his dominion. Bless the Lᴏʀᴅ, O my soul!_

My friend, we need to give ourselves a pep talk when we're grieving. We need to remind ourselves who God is and praise Him for all the good things He has done for us. David did this in Psalm 103. He reminded himself of all the benefits of God's nature and works and praised Him for them.

As you look back through this study, can you list things God has done for you? Are you able to see His work in your life as you grieve? Write about the healing you are seeing in your grief.

Just Journaling

In your Journal, summarize what you learned from your study of Psalm 103. Then, write a poem or prayer expressing your praise or simply add to your "What I Learned About God" or "Gratitude" list.

Psalm 23

Psalm 23 is often read at funerals and the bedsides of those who are ill. The truth found in this passage regarding the Good Shepherd are of great comfort for us who grieve. Spend time today digging into this passage and discover truth you can apply in your life.

Mark important phrases in a distinct way. Be sure to mark every mention of _Lord_ including synonyms and pronouns.

What does David say about the Lord? What is the result of this truth?

What does God do for us?

What else does God do and why? Does the context give us any light on what this restoration is?

Are you walking through the valley of the shadow of death? Do you feel like death is all around you in your grief? How did David respond to this?

What does God do for us with respect to our enemies?

What is David confident of?

PSALM 23

A Psalm of David.

¹ The Lord is my shepherd; I shall not want.
²   He makes me lie down in green pastures.
He leads me beside still waters.
³   He restores my soul.
He leads me in paths of righteousness
*   for his name's sake.*
⁴ Even though I walk through the valley of the shadow of death,
*   I will fear no evil,*
for you are with me;
*   your rod and your staff,*
*   they comfort me.*
⁵ You prepare a table before me
*   in the presence of my enemies;*
you anoint my head with oil;
*   my cup overflows.*
⁶ Surely goodness and mercy shall follow me
*   all the days of my life,*
and I shall dwell in the house of
*   the Lord forever.*

Do you believe that God can heal you? We often have so much pain and brokenness in grief! Are you willing to let God heal your wounds? What might that look like?

Think about what a good shepherd does for his sheep. Do you need God to do these things for you? Make a list of things you need from God when you are grieving.

Turn your list into a prayer, asking Him for the specific things you need.

Just Journaling

In your Journal, summarize what you learned from Psalm 23. Then, look back in your Journal at what you wrote about what healing might look like. Having studied God's Word, do you see God healing you in your grief? Write your own psalm of thanksgiving. Or write out a prayer asking Him to heal you and to how you what you need to do to aid in your healing.

Sheep and the Good Shepherd

Psalm 23 says the Lord is our shepherd. We are His sheep. Read Isaiah 53:6 and note what you learn about sheep.

Sheep	ISAIAH 53:6
	6 All we like sheep have gone astray; we have turned—every one—to his own way; and the Lord has laid on him the iniquity of us all.

We are all sheep that have gone astray, meaning we have all sinned. Because of our sin, we were separated from God. Jesus came to die and be raised from the dead so that we could have a relationship with God both here on earth and for eternity. Our loved ones who have died will not come back to live on earth, but we can spend eternity in heaven with them and all believers if we believe in Jesus Christ.

In John 10 Jesus teaches about sheep and the shepherd. Let's look at passages from this chapter.

First, read John 10:1-10. Underline *door* and circle *sheep*.

What does the Shepherd do?

What do the sheep do with respect to the Shepherd?

According to verses 9-10, why did Jesus come?

Why do thieves come?

JOHN 10:1-10

[1] *"Truly, truly, I say to you, he who does not enter the sheepfold by the door but climbs in by another way, that man is a thief and a robber.* [2] *But he who enters by the door is the shepherd of he sheep.* [3] *To him the gatekeeper opens. The sheep hear his voice, and he calls his own sheep by name and leads them out.* [4] *When he has brought out all his own, he goes before them, and the sheep follow him, for they know his voice.* [5] *A stranger they will not follow, but they will flee from him, for they do not know the voice of strangers."* [6] *This figure of speech Jesus used with them, but they did not understand what he was saying to them.* [7] *So Jesus again said to them, "Truly, truly, I say to you, I am the door of the sheep.* [8] *All who came before me are thieves and robbers, but the sheep did not listen to them.* [9] *I am the door. If anyone enters by me, he will be saved and will go in and out and find pasture.* [10] *The thief comes only to steal and kill and destroy. I came that they may have life and have it abundantly.*

Compare Psalm 23:2-3 to John 10:9. What do these verses say about pasture?

Now read John 10:11-18. Circle *sheep* and underline *the good shepherd*. Mark *the Father* with a triangle and draw a cross over all references to *Jesus*. Shade *hired hand* and all synonyms that refer to him.

JOHN 10:11-18

[11] *I am the good shepherd. The good shepherd lays down his life for the sheep.* [12] *He who is a hired hand and not a shepherd, who does not own the sheep, sees the wolf coming and leaves the sheep and flees, and the wolf snatches them and scatters them.* [13] *He flees because he is a hired hand and cares nothing for the sheep.* [14] *I am the good shepherd. I know my own and my own know me,* [15] *just as the Father knows me and I know the Father; and I lay down my life for the sheep.* [16] *And I have other sheep that are not of this fold. I must bring them also, and they will listen to my voice. So there will be one flock, one shepherd.* [17] *For this reason the Father loves me, because I lay down my life that I may take it up again.* [18] *No one takes it from me, but I lay it down of my own accord. I have authority to lay it down, and I have authority to take it up again. This charge I have received from my Father."*

Compare the good shepherd to the hired hand by completing this chart. Be sure to note the verses for reference.

Good Shepherd	**Hired hand**

Good Shepherd	**Hired hand**

Look back at verses 15-18. How is the relation between Jesus and the Father described?

What does Jesus do for the sheep according to these verses?

Now read John 10:25-30. Circle *sheep*. Mark *Father* with a triangle and draw a cross over all references to *Jesus*.

What does this passage say about sheep?

JOHN 10:27-30

²⁷ *My sheep hear my voice, and I know them, and they follow me.* ²⁸ *I give them eternal life, and they will never perish, and no one will snatch them out of my hand.* ²⁹ *My Father, who has given them to me, is greater than all, and no one is able to snatch them out of the Father's hand.* ³⁰ *I and the Father are one."*

What does it say about eternal life?

Summarize what you learned about sheep and their relationship with God. You have already written some of this but review is good for learning.

How can you apply what you learned from John 10 in your life?

Dear one, **if your loved ones were believers in Jesus Christ,** if they were Christians, Jesus knows them and He gave them eternal life. No one is able to snatch them out of the Father's hand. **They *are* okay;** you have no need to worry or be concerned about them. They are in the presence of Christ and will live eternally with God. **But while you are living in your earthy body, you still have work to do.**

As a child of God and believer in Christ, God's love for you is higher than the heavens. He has removed your transgressions from you as far as the east is from the west. God has redeemed you from the pit and crowns you with love and mercy. You are His sheep. All who are His sheep hear His voice and follow Him. As you follow Him and obey His commands you will be transformed into His image. **He is a good shepherd who will restore your soul even in the midst of grief and suffering.**

1 Peter 2:21-25

²¹ For to this you have been called, because Christ also suffered for you,

leaving you an example, so that you might follow in his steps.

²² He committed no sin, neither was deceit found in his mouth.

²³ When he was reviled, he did not revile in return;

when he suffered, he did not threaten,

but continued entrusting himself to him who judges justly.

²⁴ He himself bore our sins in his body on the tree,

that we might die to sin and live to righteousness.

By his wounds you have been healed.

[25] For you were straying like sheep,

but have now returned to the Shepherd and Overseer of your souls.

We are called to follow Christ and become like Him. As you grow to be like Christ through grief and suffering, will you follow His example, beloved? He bore our sins that we might die to sin and live to righteousness. Will you? He came to give us eternal life, a wonderful life that begins at the moment of salvation. You do not have to wait until you reach heaven to begin to walk in the Spirit and live by the Spirit. You can begin today. We pray you will.

Just Journaling

In your Journal, list everything you learned about the sheep and the Good Shepherd.

Then, explain how you can apply what you learned from John 10 in your life.

Finally, add to your list of "What I Learned About God." Write out a prayer of thanksgiving for all He has taught you in this study and for what He has done for you.

Wrap Up

When we were asked to write this study, our thoughts immediately turned to God and what we have in Christ. We believe that if hurting, grieving people understand God and His nature, if they understand what He has done for us and what He promises to do, they will find healing and have hope, joy, and peace in Christ.

As we have said, the loss of a loved one hurts! We feel sorrow and pain when someone we love dies. We miss so many things about them. Even so, we can have peace and joy. We can go on living and doing what God has called us to do as His sons and daughters. He will use ugly things for His glory and our good.

Dear one, you have spent precious time studying these things. You have spent the past weeks and months learning truth about God and His nature. You have learned what He has done for you and what He promises to do.

We began by reading scriptures that promise God's comfort in grief. Then we asked why we should study God's Word during our grief. The Bible is life and light to us. We can delight in the Word and find answers to our hardest questions by seeking God and studying His Word. We looked at Psalm 119 and other passages that speak of the importance of studying and applying it.

Next we learned how some people in the Bible grieved. We studied hard truths about why people die and God's sovereignty. We learned that God controls life and death. All our days were written in His book before one of them came to be. He is good, loving, compassionate, gracious, and just. He is a good Father and He is King of kings and Lord of lords. We can trust Him because of who He is.

Then we examined our behavior in grief and how we can welcome God's transformation in our lives. We looked at changing our thoughts from death and dying to life and living. We made gratitude lists and a list of what is true and noble and right and pure and lovely and commendable and excellent and praiseworthy. We learned that we must not listen to lies from the enemy but must accept the forgiveness of God when we repent of our sin. We must forgive others who hurt us in our suffering. We spent time studying about prayer and trusting God.

Along the way we made lists of what we learned about God, angels, heaven, who we are and what we have *in Christ*, how we can know we have eternal life, and other topics.

Finally, we examined passages from James regarding how we should live even during trials and suffering. And we looked at Psalms 103 and 23 to learn more about God. From John 10 we learned that if we are His sheep, we will hear His voice and follow (obey) Him.

Beloved, you may still be wrestling with some of the passages we studied. Don't give up! Keep seeking God and studying His Word; He will reveal truth to you. As you study truth and apply it in your life you will understand what the next right thing is for you to do. You will know truth and the truth will set you free even in your grief.

This week take time to look back at the lists you made. Think about all you have learned from studying God's Word. Then look at what you wrote in your *Healing in Grief Journal* about what healing will look like for you. How are you doing? Have you begun to see God's healing in your life?

Look through each lesson in this study. Write one truth you want to remember from each lesson.

Lesson 1

Lesson 2

Lesson 3

Lesson 4

Lesson 5

Lesson 6

Lesson 7

Lesson 8

Lesson 9

Lesson 10

Lesson 11

Lesson 12

Lesson 13

Lesson 14

Lesson 15

Lesson 16

Lesson 17

Lesson 18

One last *Just Journaling* prompt:

Just Journaling

What are some of the things you want to take away from this study? How has this study helped you in your grief?

Where are you today compared to where you were when you started this study? Have you seen God's healing in your grief? Thank Him for all He is doing in and through you.

Epilogue

[Ron] Before The Accident, we had experienced a few challenges, not as bad as some people face but worse than others. We had some experience with death, having lost my parents and in-laws to illnesses. We had some experience with personal suffering from physical ailments. Perhaps most challenging, we'd raised seven children, some of whom had struggled with "adulting." We saw them practice self-destructive behaviors with zeal, creativity, and perseverance. That's not how God intended those traits to be directed. We found these episodes very difficult.

Nothing, however, compared to losing Andrew. He was happy and successful, loving his life and seemingly on-track for a beautiful future. It was devastating!

But God. As the Bible says in a few places, "But God." But God showed Himself strong. But God was truly a "very present help in trouble" (Psalm 46:1). We were "dead" in our grief and discouragement and shame and fear and anger . . . but God made us alive together in Christ. Because of His great love and by His grace we experienced His salvation life as we walked this path. We were and are convinced that we have a good and beautiful God. Accordingly, we have a good and beautiful life, an eternal kind of life that started with our meeting Him. We're convinced Jesus is Immanuel, "God with us," here and now. We're convinced that the Kingdom of Heaven is "now at hand" as Jesus said repeatedly.

> **But God, being rich in mercy,**
>
> **Because of the great love with which he loved us,**
>
> **Even when we were dead in our trespasses**
>
> **Made us alive together with Christ –**
>
> **by grace you have been saved**
>
> **(Ephesians 2:4-5)**

And yet, our son was dead. We knew life included suffering, even for Christians. That's very clear in the Bible. In fact, I had no rational objection to the fact that bad things happen to good people. However, I had a semiconscious assumption that this would always be other good people. It took some time and willingness to reconcile our experience of the eternal kind of life in Christ with the hard evidence that our beautiful son was dead.

We have found that biblical truths have to work their way from our head to our heart. This is no passive process enabled simply by gravity or time. No, it takes walking through fire and pressure while facing the right direction, walking meaning we keep going, we try again, we don't give up completely. And facing the right direction, meaning we gratefully look to our good and loving God as our source and His Word as our guide. It takes walking-out this faith, this relationship with God, in our daily life.

We are learning biblical truths we thought we already understood. We are finding ugly things in our heart we thought were gone: things like selfishness, fear, resentment, pride, and laziness. Suffering does in fact often bring a peculiar clarity. I had a growing realization of ways I had failed as a father and husband that clearly contributed to my family's struggles. Fortunately, none of this surprises God; He already knew that stuff was there and had the power to deal with it. He guides us to repent, ask forgiveness, and make amends to our family. So, though this may sound odd, we are in some ways better off now. Our other children are much better off than they were three years ago as well. They are beautiful adults who are glorifying God, living well, and helping others.

We found that life with Christ is a beautiful journey. Sadness and grief remain, but they do not reign.

[Kathleen] Like many of you I have experienced the loss of people I love. My mother died of liver disease when I was only 34 years old. Just eight years later my father died from heart disease. Over the next six years I helped care for my in-laws as they each died from cancer. In 2013 our twenty-year-old son was killed in a drunk driving incident I refer to as "The Accident." I have lost other family members and friends to illness, addiction, accidents, and suicide.

Each time we lost a family member we had to deal with paperwork, make travel plans, and make decisions about funerals and their personal items. We had to tell our children that their grandparent, aunt, friend, or brother was gone. We had to figure out how to handle our loss while helping others grieve as well.

The loss of our son was the hardest loss. It cut me to the core of my being. Even so, I have found healing.

As I look back over those first three years since my son died I am struck by how raw my wound was and how excruciating daily living was in the early days of my grief journey. I see the pain, the sorrow, and intense grief I experienced in those first months. I see how simple tasks were extremely difficult. Just getting out of bed or going to the store was hard.

I am in awe that I no longer walk in that pain. I no longer walk in a fog of constant sorrow and grief. I have joy, peace, and hope that could only have come from seeking God and applying His Word in my grief. I lifted my eyes to the hills and my help came from the Lord who made heaven and earth. When I needed comfort at odd hours of the day and night it was reassuring and comforting to know that God does not slumber or sleep. He was and is my Keeper; He is my Shade on my right hand. He has kept me from evil and he is keeping my life. I know the Lord will keep my going out and my coming in from this time forth and forevermore. I also know He keeps those I love who are also His children from this time forth and forevermore.

Each loss left a void in my life. There is a void that only Andrew filled. I miss his laugh, his stomping through the house, his hugs, and his stories. Nothing will ever replace my son in my life. I still have moments and even days of sadness. Some memories still bring tears. I hate that his niece and nephews won't know him like they will know their other uncles and aunts. Yes, I will grieve my son until I die.

However, those early days of sorrow so deep that I physically ached are gone. The days of doubt, sobbing, and aching have passed. Seeing an old picture of all four of my boys together no longer takes my breath away. I no longer count the days, weeks, or months since I saw him last or since the date of his death. I no longer cry each time I see a picture of him or hear his name. I no longer wake up with my pillow soaked with my tears. Death is no longer a central theme in my thoughts. Hope and joy are central in my life now.

Pictures and stories of family members who are no longer here on earth bring smiles rather than tears. I enjoy looking back at old photos and seeing my parents and in-laws with our children. I enjoy hearing stories of their antics. I rejoice at seeing my son's friends growing and living. I love that my adult children mention their grandparents fondly and still tell stories of their brother.

Friends, family, and, of course, grandchildren bring me joy. I have peace, a peace that can only come from God. I sleep well. Sometimes I dream of Andrew and others I have lost, and I am glad. I know they are simply dreams, not messages from them, but the dreams are still sweet. I ride my bicycle with friends, travel with my husband, and mow our property with my tractor. I read great books, study my Bible, and enjoy movies. I play with my dogs, visit with friends, and go out to eat. In short, I live.

I live a joyful, peaceful life despite my losses. God is using the trials of this life to mold me and transform me into the image of His Son. The transformation is uncomfortable at times but it is wonderful even still. I know He will do the same for you as you seek Him, study His Word and apply it in your life, and do the next right thing.

I know I have forgotten things about Andrew and my other family members, stories they told, little things. I see pictures and wish they were here to tell me the backstory. I miss my parents and in-laws. There are times I wish I could pick up the phone and speak with them about things in my life. I miss Andrew. Though I have forgotten little things about them, I know they lived. They lived well. They still live. Because each of them believed that Jesus is the son of God, was crucified for our sins, died, was buried and rose on the third day, though their bodies are buried in the ground, they are now in the presence of Christ and someday I will join them there. Though people on earth may forget them, their names are written in the Lamb's Book of Life because they were followers of Jesus.

My heart is no longer broken. I no longer think of death, dying, grief, and pain much of the time. Yes, there is a void. Yes, there is a scar. Yes, I have experienced loss. But in Christ I have found peace, joy, and strength to go forth and do the next right thing. I am God's workmanship, created in Christ Jesus to do good works which God prepared in advance for me to do. I am willing to do those good works. I will live and work as unto the Lord until my appointed time to die.

As you work through your grief and seek God, you don't have to figure out tomorrow or next week, just do what He has called you to do today. As you seek God and as He works in you, you, too, will find healing, peace, and joy. You can have hope in Christ Jesus and experience God's healing in your grief.

****

As I type this, I am in tears. A dear friend is at home with the Lord. After a four-year battle with brain cancer, Jathan went Home this morning. He was full of love, joy, and hope. He loves Jesus and now sees Him face to face in all of His glory. His family now faces life without this precious husband and father. We, their friends, are reaching out to love and support them through their grief. God is near to the brokenhearted and will comfort Keli. She and I have had many deep conversations about the Lord and death this past year. She has seen in us God's healing in grief.

It is for Jathan's family and for all who grieve that we wrote this book. Our prayer is that you all find God's healing in grief.

Using This Book
for Group Discussions

This book is a great tool for small-group study involving people who are interested in learning for themselves more about what the Bible says about God's healing in grief.

The group will need a leader who is comfortable facilitating discussion; it is best if the leader has not just started their grief journey. All participants should complete each lesson's study activities on their own before the group meets.

You may want to allow about an hour to an hour and a half for each class. Provide time for each person to verbalize their answers and discoveries; encourage everyone to contribute to the discussion. Keep the focus on what the Bible says. Discussing insights drawn from what God says about the subjects in this book will help people heal as they apply these life-impacting truths.

Remember the focus of discussion must remain on the truth found in Bible, not what the class members are feeling that day or on any individual's loss. The leader may need to gently steer the class back to the material in the book if someone gets off track. Some in your class may need reminders of the purpose of the class—to learn truth from God's Word and how to apply it. It is in seeking God, studying truth, and applying it that we find healing in grief.

If you are the leader…

Always open and close your time together in prayer.

In the first class meeting you may want to give participants a few moments to introduce themselves. Limit this to a few sentences; this is not the time to share all about their loved ones' deaths. After introductions, give the class a quick tour of the book and show them how to use it; explain the layout and order of the lessons. Show your class how to mark the scriptures in the sidebar. You may want to work through one or two passages with them as examples. Be sure the group understands that their participation in discussion is beneficial for everyone but that the discussion will focus on answers found in God's Word. Explain the *Just Journaling* prompts and encourage them to write their answers in their own *Journal*. Be sure to tell you group that their answers to the *Just Journaling* prompts are for their use only. They will not be asked to share their Journals with the class if they don't want to do so.

Each week you will discuss a lesson or two depending on your time and the needs of the group. It is best to decide ahead of time whether you will be completing one lesson per week or two. Remember that some lessons will be harder than others; some class members may struggle with particular lessons. Encourage them to work through as much of the lesson as they can and come to class even if they do not complete all of the homework. Group members will be strengthened by the class discussion and time spent with other believers, so everyone should come even if they do not have the homework completed.

As the leader your job is to facilitate your students' discussion of what they learned, not to lecture or tell them all you know. You need to do all of the homework and plan ahead which questions you want to discuss in class. When you ask a question, be sure to allow time for others to answer before offering your views. It is easy to dominate the discussion when leading a class like this. Don't give in to that temptation! If no one in the class answers your question, ask it in a different way and give them time to think about their answers. The goal of the leader is to help others understand truth for themselves. Verbalizing what they have learned will help others learn and will solidify truth in their hearts and minds.

You may want to encourage your class to find time in addition to class discussion time, to get together for encouragement. Grief can be lonely and it is easy for people to isolate themselves. The class can be a means for developing long-lasting friendships between people who have come through a difficult time and together have found healing, hope, peace, and joy by seeking God, studying and applying His Word, and doing the next right thing.

Helpful Resources

Arthur, Kay. *When the Hurt Runs Deep*. Colorado Springs, CO: WaterBrook Press, 2010.

Arthur, Kay, and Bob and Diane Vereen. *Heaven, Hell, and Life After Death*. Colorado Springs, CO: WaterBrook Press, 2014.

Chapman, Mary Beth, and Ellen Vaughn. *Choosing to SEE: A Journey of Struggle and Hope*. Grand Rapids, MI: Revell, 2010.

Duncan, Kathleen B. *My Journey through Grief into Grace*. Wichita Falls, TX: R and K Publishing, 2015.

Duncan, Kathleen B. *What Bereaved Parents Want You to Know (But May Not Say)*. Wichita Falls, TX: R and K Publishing, 2015.

Elliot, Elisabeth. *A Path Through Suffering: Discovering the Relationship Between God's Mercy and Our Pain*. Grand Rapids, MI: Revell, 2014.

Gillaspie, Pam. *Sweeter Than Chocolate! An Inductive Study of Psalm 119*. Chattanooga, TN: Precept Ministries International, 2009.

Guthrie, David and Nancy Guthrie. *When Your Family's Lost a Loved One: Finding Hope Together*. Colorado Springs, CO: Focus on the Family Publishing, 2008.

Keller, Timothy. *Walking with God through Pain and Suffering*. New York: Riverhead Books, an imprint of Penguin Random House LLC, 2015.

Laurie, Greg. *Hope for Hurting Hearts*. Dana Point, CA: Kerygma/Allen David Publishing, 2010.

Lusko, Levi. *Through the Eyes of a Lion*. Nashville, TN: W Publishing Group, an imprint of Thomas Nelson, 2015.

Parrish, Preston and Glenda Parrish. *Finding Hope in Times of Grief*. Eugene, OR: Harvest House Publishers, 2011.

Saake, Jennifer. *Hannah's Hope: Seeking God's Heart in the Midst of Infertility, Miscarriage, and Adoption Loss*. Colorado Springs, CO: NavPress, 2005.

Sittser, Jerry L. *A Grace Disguised*. Grand Rapids, MI: Zondervan, 2004.